# TEACHER'S PET PUBLICATIONS

PUZZLE PACK
for
Johnny Tremain

based on the book by
Esther Forbes

Written by
William T. Collins

© 2005 Teacher's Pet Publications
All Rights Reserved

The materials in this packet are copyrighted
by Teacher's Pet Publications, Inc.

These pages may be duplicated by the purchaser
for use in the purchaser's own classroom.

Copying any of these materials and distributing them
for any other purpose is a violation of the copyright laws.

© 2005 Teacher's Pet Publications, Inc.
www.tpet.com

INTRODUCTION
If you already own the LitPlan for this title, this Puzzle Pack will refresh your Unit Resource Materials and Vocabulary Resource Materials sections plus give you additional materials you can substitute into the tests. If you do not already have a complete LitPlan, these pages will give you some supplemental materials to use with your own plan. There are two main groups of materials: one set for unit words (such as characters' names, symbols, places, etc.) and one set for vocabulary words associated with the book.

WORD LIST
There is a word list for both the unit words and the vocabulary words. These lists show you which words are being used in the materials and the clues or definitions being used for those words. You may want to give students a word list with clues/definitions to help them, or you may want students to only have a word list (without clues/definitions) if you want them to work a little harder. Both are available for duplication. The word lists can also be your "calling key" for the bingo games.

FILL IN THE BLANK AND MATCHING
There are 4 each of the fill in the blank and matching worksheets for both the unit and vocabulary words. These pages can be used either as extra worksheets for students or as objective parts of a unit test. They can be done individually if students need extra help or as a whole class activity to review the material covered.

MAGIC SQUARES
The magic squares not only reinforce the material covered but also work on reasoning and math skills. Many teachers have told us that their students really enjoy doing these!

WORD SEARCH PUZZLES
The word search words go in all directions, as indicated on your answer keys. Two of the word search puzzles have the clues listed rather than the words. This makes the puzzle a little more difficult, but it reinforces the material better. Two word search puzzles have words only for students who find the clue puzzles too difficult.

CROSSWORD PUZZLES
Both unit and vocabulary word sections have 4 crossword puzzles.

BINGO CARDS
There are 32 individual bingo cards for the unit words and 32 individual bingo cards for the vocabulary words. You can use your word list as a "call list," calling the words at random and marking them off of your list as you go, or you could use the flash cards by cutting them apart and drawing the words at random from a hat (or box or whatever). To make a better review, you might ask for the definition and spelling of each word as you call it out–or you could call out the definitions and have students tell you the words they need to look for on the puzzle.

JUGGLE LETTERS
The vocabulary juggle letter game is intended to help students learn the spellings of the words. One sheet has the definitions listed on it as an extra help for students who need it or to reinforce the definitions if you choose to do so.

FLASH CARDS
We've included a set of vocabulary flash cards you can duplicate, cut, and fold for your students. Some teachers make a few sets for general use by the class; others make a set for each student. Some teachers duplicate them for each student and have the students cut & fold their own. You can cut out just the words and put them in a hat, have each student pick out one word and write the definition and a sentence for that word. Students then swap words and papers, with the next student adding a sentence of his own under the last one. You can have students swap as many times as you like. Each time the student will read the sentences written prior to his own and then add a sentence. You can cut out the words and definitions separately and play "I Have; Who Has?" Each student in the room draws a word and definition. The first student says, "I have (the name of the word). Who has the definition?" The student with the definition reads it then says, "I have (the name of the vocabulary word she has). Who has the definition?" The round continues until all words and definitions have been given.

Johnny Tremain Unit Word List

Word	Clue/Definition
1. ADAMS	Main speaker at Observer Club meetings
2. BESSIE	Daughter of Liberty
3. BILLY	Pretended to be drunk to leave the city
4. BOSTON	Setting of the novel
5. CHARLESTOWN	General Gage took the cannon and gunpowder from there
6. CILLA	Lapham daughter intended to marry Johnny
7. CONCORD	Town near Lexington
8. COOPER	Preached more about politics than God
9. DOODLE	Patriotic song; Yankee ___
10. DORCAS	Ran off with Frizel, Junior
11. DOVE	Gave Johnny a broken crucible
12. DRAGON	Meeting place for artisans in spy network: Green ___
13. DUSTY	Apprentice who was afraid of Johnny
14. ENGLAND	Owner of the colonies
15. FORBES	Author
16. GAGE	Took supplies from Charlestown
17. GOBLIN	Johnny's horse
18. HANCOCK	Wealthy merchant, ordered sugar basin from Mr. Lapham
19. HARBOR	Where the tea was thrown: Boston ___
20. HOPPER	Midwife who tended Johnny's burned hand
21. ISANNAH	Attracted many because of her frail nature
22. JAMES	Said that a man can stand up
23. JOHNNY	Silversmith apprentice turned rebel
24. LAPHAM	Owned silversmith shop
25. LATOUR	Johnny's father: Dr. Charles ___
26. LAVINIA	Made Isannah her protegee
27. LEXINGTON	Site of first shot of Revolutionary War
28. LIBERTY	Leaders in the revolt against England: Sons of ___
29. LORNE	Owned Boston Observer
30. LYTE	Greedy merchant: Jonathan ___
31. MADGE	Married a British soldier
32. MINUTE	Colonial army: ___ Men
33. MONTAGUE	Said citizens would pay the fiddler: Admiral ___
34. NEWMAN	Hung the lanterns in Christ Church
35. OBSERVER	Newspaper that printed articles about revolt
36. PUMPKIN	Gave his musket to Johny
37. QUEEN	Popular Boston restaurant: Afric ___
38. QUINCY	Lawyer who defended Johnny for free
39. RAB	First to hear Johnny's story
40. REVERE	Warned Lexington and Concord of battle
41. SILVERSMITH	Johnny's first occupation
42. SMITH	In charge of British troops at battle in Lexington
43. STRANGER	Taught Johnny to ride a horse
44. TEA	Colonists refused to pay tax on it
45. TORIES	They were loyal to England
46. TWEEDIE	Silversmith from Baltimore: Percival ___
47. WARREN	Treated Johnny's burned hand
48. WHIGS	Wanted freedom from England

Copyrighted

Johnny Tremain Fill In The Blank 1

_____	1. In charge of British troops at battle in Lexington
_____	2. Johnny's father: Dr. Charles ___
_____	3. First to hear Johnny's story
_____	4. Colonists refused to pay tax on it
_____	5. Wanted freedom from England
_____	6. Silversmith from Baltimore: Percival ___
_____	7. Midwife who tended Johnny's burned hand
_____	8. Preached more about politics than God
_____	9. Taught Johnny to ride a horse
_____	10. Owned Boston Observer
_____	11. Popular Boston restaurant: Afric ___
_____	12. Gave his musket to Johny
_____	13. Greedy merchant: Jonathan ___
_____	14. Treated Johnny's burned hand
_____	15. Attracted many because of her frail nature
_____	16. Took supplies from Charlestown
_____	17. Meeting place for artisans in spy network: Green ___
_____	18. Said that a man can stand up
_____	19. Setting of the novel
_____	20. Site of first shot of Revolutionary War

Johnny Tremain Fill In The Blank 1 Answer Key

SMITH	1. In charge of British troops at battle in Lexington
LATOUR	2. Johnny's father: Dr. Charles ___
RAB	3. First to hear Johnny's story
TEA	4. Colonists refusted to pay tax on it
WHIGS	5. Wanted freedom from England
TWEEDIE	6. Silversmith from Baltimore: Percival ___
HOPPER	7. Midwife who tended Johnny's burned hand
COOPER	8. Preached more about politics than God
STRANGER	9. Taught Johnny to ride a horse
LORNE	10. Owned Boston Observer
QUEEN	11. Popular Boston restaurant: Afric ___
PUMPKIN	12. Gave his musket to Johny
LYTE	13. Greedy merchant: Jonathan ___
WARREN	14. Treated Johnny's burned hand
ISANNAH	15. Attracted many because of her frail nature
GAGE	16. Took supplies from Charlestown
DRAGON	17. Meeting place for artisans in spy network: Green ___
JAMES	18. Said that a man can stand up
BOSTON	19. Setting of the novel
LEXINGTON	20. Site of first shot of Revolutionary War

Johnny Tremain Fill In The Blank 2

_____ 1. Owned Boston Observer

_____ 2. In charge of British troops at battle in Lexington

_____ 3. Married a British soldier

_____ 4. Silversmith from Baltimore: Percival ___

_____ 5. Warned Lexington and Concord of battle

_____ 6. Site of first shot of Revolutionary War

_____ 7. First to hear Johnny's story

_____ 8. Apprentice who was afraid of Johnny

_____ 9. Hung the lanterns in Christ Church

_____ 10. Where the tea was thrown: Boston ___

_____ 11. Johnny's horse

_____ 12. Owner of the colonies

_____ 13. Setting of the novel

_____ 14. Lapham daughter intended to marry Johnny

_____ 15. Newspaper that printed articles about revolt

_____ 16. They were loyal to England

_____ 17. Colonists refused to pay tax on it

_____ 18. Took supplies from Charlestown

_____ 19. Gave Johnny a broken crucible

_____ 20. Town near Lexington

Johnny Tremain Fill In The Blank 2 Answer Key

Answer	#	Clue
LORNE	1.	Owned Boston Observer
SMITH	2.	In charge of British troops at battle in Lexington
MADGE	3.	Married a British soldier
TWEEDIE	4.	Silversmith from Baltimore: Percival ___
REVERE	5.	Warned Lexington and Concord of battle
LEXINGTON	6.	Site of first shot of Revolutionary War
RAB	7.	First to hear Johnny's story
DUSTY	8.	Apprentice who was afraid of Johnny
NEWMAN	9.	Hung the lanterns in Christ Church
HARBOR	10.	Where the tea was thrown: Boston ___
GOBLIN	11.	Johnny's horse
ENGLAND	12.	Owner of the colonies
BOSTON	13.	Setting of the novel
CILLA	14.	Lapham daughter intended to marry Johnny
OBSERVER	15.	Newspaper that printed articles about revolt
TORIES	16.	They were loyal to England
TEA	17.	Colonists refused to pay tax on it
GAGE	18.	Took supplies from Charlestown
DOVE	19.	Gave Johnny a broken crucible
CONCORD	20.	Town near Lexington

Johnny Tremain Fill In The Blank 3

1. Gave Johnny a broken crucible
2. Preached more about politics than God
3. Attracted many because of her frail nature
4. First to hear Johnny's story
5. Made Isannah her protegee
6. Said citizens would pay the fiddler: Admiral ___
7. Owned silversmith shop
8. Colonists refused to pay tax on it
9. Married a British soldier
10. Silversmith apprentice turned rebel
11. Silversmith from Baltimore: Percival ___
12. Newspaper that printed articles about revolt
13. Main speaker at Observer Club meetings
14. Taught Johnny to ride a horse
15. Meeting place for artisans in spy network: Green ___
16. General Gage took the cannon and gunpowder from there
17. Daughter of Liberty
18. Leaders in the revolt against England: Sons of ___
19. In charge of British troops at battle in Lexington
20. Site of first shot of Revolutionary War

Johnny Tremain Fill In The Blank 3 Answer Key

DOVE	1. Gave Johnny a broken crucible
COOPER	2. Preached more about politics than God
ISANNAH	3. Attracted many because of her frail nature
RAB	4. First to hear Johnny's story
LAVINIA	5. Made Isannah her protegee
MONTAGUE	6. Said citizens would pay the fiddler: Admiral ___
LAPHAM	7. Owned silversmith shop
TEA	8. Colonists refused to pay tax on it
MADGE	9. Married a British soldier
JOHNNY	10. Silversmith apprentice turned rebel
TWEEDIE	11. Silversmith from Baltimore: Percival ___
OBSERVER	12. Newspaper that printed articles about revolt
ADAMS	13. Main speaker at Observer Club meetings
STRANGER	14. Taught Johnny to ride a horse
DRAGON	15. Meeting place for artisans in spy network: Green ___
CHARLESTOWN	16. General Gage took the cannon and gunpowder from there
BESSIE	17. Daughter of Liberty
LIBERTY	18. Leaders in the revolt against England: Sons of ___
SMITH	19. In charge of British troops at battle in Lexington
LEXINGTON	20. Site of first shot of Revolutionary War

Johnny Tremain Fill In The Blank 4

1. Patriotic song; Yankee ___
2. Taught Johnny to ride a horse
3. Said that a man can stand up
4. They were loyal to England
5. Owned Boston Observer
6. Treated Johnny's burned hand
7. Married a British soldier
8. Pretended to be drunk to leave the city
9. Silversmith apprentice turned rebel
10. Johnny's horse
11. Gave his musket to Johny
12. Town near Lexington
13. Said citizens would pay the fiddler: Admiral ___
14. Popular Boston restaurant: Afric ___
15. Took supplies from Charlestown
16. Greedy merchant: Jonathan ___
17. Setting of the novel
18. Daughter of Liberty
19. Leaders in the revolt against England: Sons of ___
20. Johnny's first occupation

Johnny Tremain Fill In The Blank 4 Answer Key

DOODLE	1. Patriotic song; Yankee ___
STRANGER	2. Taught Johnny to ride a horse
JAMES	3. Said that a man can stand up
TORIES	4. They were loyal to England
LORNE	5. Owned Boston Observer
WARREN	6. Treated Johnny's burned hand
MADGE	7. Married a British soldier
BILLY	8. Pretended to be drunk to leave the city
JOHNNY	9. Silversmith apprentice turned rebel
GOBLIN	10. Johnny's horse
PUMPKIN	11. Gave his musket to Johny
CONCORD	12. Town near Lexington
MONTAGUE	13. Said citizens would pay the fiddler: Admiral ___
QUEEN	14. Popular Boston restaurant: Afric ___
GAGE	15. Took supplies from Charlestown
LYTE	16. Greedy merchant: Jonathan ___
BOSTON	17. Setting of the novel
BESSIE	18. Daughter of Liberty
LIBERTY	19. Leaders in the revolt against England: Sons of ___
SILVERSMITH	20. Johnny's first occupation

Johnny Tremain Matching 1

___ 1. BESSIE   A. Daughter of Liberty
___ 2. QUINCY   B. Lawyer who defended Johnny for free
___ 3. WHIGS   C. Said that a man can stand up
___ 4. OBSERVER   D. Midwife who tended Johnny's burned hand
___ 5. COOPER   E. Johnny's first occupation
___ 6. SILVERSMITH   F. Silversmith from Baltimore: Percival ___
___ 7. DOVE   G. Wealthy merchant, ordered sugar basin from Mr. Lapham
___ 8. STRANGER   H. Silversmith apprentice turned rebel
___ 9. RAB   I. Johnny's horse
___10. TWEEDIE   J. Colonial army: ___ Men
___11. REVERE   K. Preached more about politics than God
___12. ENGLAND   L. Newspaper that printed articles about revolt
___13. CHARLESTOWN   M. Wanted freedom from England
___14. JAMES   N. Warned Lexington and Concord of battle
___15. MINUTE   O. Leaders in the revolt against England: Sons of ____
___16. HANCOCK   P. Owner of the colonies
___17. LORNE   Q. Colonists refused to pay tax on it
___18. TORIES   R. First to hear Johnny's story
___19. LIBERTY   S. They were loyal to England
___20. JOHNNY   T. Taught Johnny to ride a horse
___21. GOBLIN   U. General Gage took the cannon and gunpowder from there
___22. TEA   V. Gave Johnny a broken crucible
___23. BILLY   W. Patriotic song; Yankee ___
___24. HOPPER   X. Pretended to be drunk to leave the city
___25. DOODLE   Y. Owned Boston Observer

Johnny Tremain Matching 1 Answer Key

A - 1. BESSIE	A. Daughter of Liberty
B - 2. QUINCY	B. Lawyer who defended Johnny for free
M - 3. WHIGS	C. Said that a man can stand up
L - 4. OBSERVER	D. Midwife who tended Johnny's burned hand
K - 5. COOPER	E. Johnny's first occupation
E - 6. SILVERSMITH	F. Silversmith from Baltimore: Percival ___
V - 7. DOVE	G. Wealthy merchant, ordered sugar basin from Mr. Lapham
T - 8. STRANGER	H. Silversmith apprentice turned rebel
R - 9. RAB	I. Johnny's horse
F - 10. TWEEDIE	J. Colonial army: ___ Men
N - 11. REVERE	K. Preached more about politics than God
P - 12. ENGLAND	L. Newspaper that printed articles about revolt
U - 13. CHARLESTOWN	M. Wanted freedom from England
C - 14. JAMES	N. Warned Lexington and Concord of battle
J - 15. MINUTE	O. Leaders in the revolt against England: Sons of ___
G - 16. HANCOCK	P. Owner of the colonies
Y - 17. LORNE	Q. Colonists refused to pay tax on it
S - 18. TORIES	R. First to hear Johnny's story
O - 19. LIBERTY	S. They were loyal to England
H - 20. JOHNNY	T. Taught Johnny to ride a horse
I - 21. GOBLIN	U. General Gage took the cannon and gunpowder from there
Q - 22. TEA	V. Gave Johnny a broken crucible
X - 23. BILLY	W. Patriotic song; Yankee ___
D - 24. HOPPER	X. Pretended to be drunk to leave the city
W - 25. DOODLE	Y. Owned Boston Observer

Johnny Tremain Matching 2

___ 1. ENGLAND   A. Preached more about politics than God
___ 2. RAB   B. Made Isannah her protegee
___ 3. REVERE   C. Patriotic song; Yankee ___
___ 4. LAVINIA   D. Warned Lexington and Concord of battle
___ 5. CONCORD   E. Gave his musket to Johny
___ 6. SILVERSMITH   F. Popular Boston restaurant: Afric ___
___ 7. WHIGS   G. Leaders in the revolt against England: Sons of ____
___ 8. STRANGER   H. First to hear Johnny's story
___ 9. COOPER   I. Ran off with Frizel, Junior
___10. BESSIE   J. Daughter of Liberty
___11. DRAGON   K. Midwife who tended Johnny's burned hand
___12. DOODLE   L. Owner of the colonies
___13. SMITH   M. Johnny's first occupation
___14. OBSERVER   N. Author
___15. DOVE   O. Taught Johnny to ride a horse
___16. GAGE   P. Gave Johnny a broken crucible
___17. DORCAS   Q. Wanted freedom from England
___18. FORBES   R. In charge of British troops at battle in Lexington
___19. ADAMS   S. They were loyal to England
___20. TORIES   T. Town near Lexington
___21. LATOUR   U. Johnny's father: Dr. Charles ___
___22. QUEEN   V. Main speaker at Observer Club meetings
___23. PUMPKIN   W. Meeting place for artisans in spy network: Green ___
___24. LIBERTY   X. Took supplies from Charlestown
___25. HOPPER   Y. Newspaper that printed articles about revolt

Johnny Tremain Matching 2 Answer Key

L - 1. ENGLAND	A.	Preached more about politics than God
H - 2. RAB	B.	Made Isannah her protegee
D - 3. REVERE	C.	Patriotic song; Yankee ___
B - 4. LAVINIA	D.	Warned Lexington and Concord of battle
T - 5. CONCORD	E.	Gave his musket to Johny
M - 6. SILVERSMITH	F.	Popular Boston restaurant: Afric ___
Q - 7. WHIGS	G.	Leaders in the revolt against England: Sons of ___
O - 8. STRANGER	H.	First to hear Johnny's story
A - 9. COOPER	I.	Ran off with Frizel, Junior
J - 10. BESSIE	J.	Daughter of Liberty
W - 11. DRAGON	K.	Midwife who tended Johnny's burned hand
C - 12. DOODLE	L.	Owner of the colonies
R - 13. SMITH	M.	Johnny's first occupation
Y - 14. OBSERVER	N.	Author
P - 15. DOVE	O.	Taught Johnny to ride a horse
X - 16. GAGE	P.	Gave Johnny a broken crucible
I - 17. DORCAS	Q.	Wanted freedom from England
N - 18. FORBES	R.	In charge of British troops at battle in Lexington
V - 19. ADAMS	S.	They were loyal to England
S - 20. TORIES	T.	Town near Lexington
U - 21. LATOUR	U.	Johnny's father: Dr. Charles ___
F - 22. QUEEN	V.	Main speaker at Observer Club meetings
E - 23. PUMPKIN	W.	Meeting place for artisans in spy network: Green ___
G - 24. LIBERTY	X.	Took supplies from Charlestown
K - 25. HOPPER	Y.	Newspaper that printed articles about revolt

Johnny Tremain Matching 3

___ 1. TWEEDIE   A. Newspaper that printed articles about revolt
___ 2. SMITH   B. Popular Boston restaurant: Afric ___
___ 3. DOODLE   C. Patriotic song; Yankee ___
___ 4. QUINCY   D. Gave his musket to Johny
___ 5. LIBERTY   E. Lapham daughter intended to marry Johnny
___ 6. LAVINIA   F. Leaders in the revolt against England: Sons of ____
___ 7. PUMPKIN   G. Warned Lexington and Concord of battle
___ 8. REVERE   H. Lawyer who defended Johnny for free
___ 9. OBSERVER   I. Silversmith apprentice turned rebel
___10. DORCAS   J. In charge of British troops at battle in Lexington
___11. ISANNAH   K. General Gage took the cannon and gunpowder from there
___12. MINUTE   L. Attracted many because of her frail nature
___13. HANCOCK   M. Made Isannah her protegee
___14. QUEEN   N. Owned silversmith shop
___15. MONTAGUE   O. Said citizens would pay the fiddler: Admiral ___
___16. BILLY   P. Wealthy merchant, ordered sugar basin from Mr. Lapham
___17. GOBLIN   Q. Johnny's first occupation
___18. FORBES   R. Colonial army: ___ Men
___19. SILVERSMITH   S. Pretended to be drunk to leave the city
___20. TORIES   T. They were loyal to England
___21. CHARLESTOWN   U. Author
___22. GAGE   V. Johnny's horse
___23. JOHNNY   W. Ran off with Frizel, Junior
___24. LAPHAM   X. Took supplies from Charlestown
___25. CILLA   Y. Silversmith from Baltimore: Percival ___

Johnny Tremain Matching 3 Answer Key

Y - 1. TWEEDIE   A. Newspaper that printed articles about revolt
J - 2. SMITH   B. Popular Boston restaurant: Afric ____
C - 3. DOODLE   C. Patriotic song; Yankee ____
H - 4. QUINCY   D. Gave his musket to Johny
F - 5. LIBERTY   E. Lapham daughter intended to marry Johnny
M - 6. LAVINIA   F. Leaders in the revolt against England: Sons of ____
D - 7. PUMPKIN   G. Warned Lexington and Concord of battle
G - 8. REVERE   H. Lawyer who defended Johnny for free
A - 9. OBSERVER   I. Silversmith apprentice turned rebel
W -10. DORCAS   J. In charge of British troops at battle in Lexington
L -11. ISANNAH   K. General Gage took the cannon and gunpowder from there
R -12. MINUTE   L. Attracted many because of her frail nature
P -13. HANCOCK   M. Made Isannah her protegee
B -14. QUEEN   N. Owned silversmith shop
O -15. MONTAGUE   O. Said citizens would pay the fiddler: Admiral ____
S -16. BILLY   P. Wealthy merchant, ordered sugar basin from Mr. Lapham
V -17. GOBLIN   Q. Johnny's first occupation
U -18. FORBES   R. Colonial army: ____ Men
Q -19. SILVERSMITH   S. Pretended to be drunk to leave the city
T -20. TORIES   T. They were loyal to England
K -21. CHARLESTOWN   U. Author
X -22. GAGE   V. Johnny's horse
I - 23. JOHNNY   W. Ran off with Frizel, Junior
N -24. LAPHAM   X. Took supplies from Charlestown
E -25. CILLA   Y. Silversmith from Baltimore: Percival ____

Johnny Tremain Matching 4

___ 1. GAGE   A. Patriotic song; Yankee ___
___ 2. OBSERVER   B. Silversmith apprentice turned rebel
___ 3. JAMES   C. Midwife who tended Johnny's burned hand
___ 4. LIBERTY   D. Newspaper that printed articles about revolt
___ 5. PUMPKIN   E. Made Isannah her protegee
___ 6. JOHNNY   F. Daughter of Liberty
___ 7. DORCAS   G. Took supplies from Charlestown
___ 8. BESSIE   H. Said citizens would pay the fiddler: Admiral ___
___ 9. LAPHAM   I. Preached more about politics than God
___10. QUINCY   J. Wanted freedom from England
___11. TORIES   K. Leaders in the revolt against England: Sons of ____
___12. CHARLESTOWN   L. General Gage took the cannon and gunpowder from there
___13. LAVINIA   M. They were loyal to England
___14. QUEEN   N. Warned Lexington and Concord of battle
___15. COOPER   O. Popular Boston restaurant: Afric ___
___16. BOSTON   P. Colonists refused to pay tax on it
___17. CONCORD   Q. Owned Boston Observer
___18. WHIGS   R. Setting of the novel
___19. DOODLE   S. Lawyer who defended Johnny for free
___20. TEA   T. Said that a man can stand up
___21. MONTAGUE   U. Town near Lexington
___22. REVERE   V. Gave his musket to Johny
___23. LORNE   W. Site of first shot of Revolutionary War
___24. HOPPER   X. Ran off with Frizel, Junior
___25. LEXINGTON   Y. Owned silversmith shop

Johnny Tremain Matching 4 Answer Key

G - 1.	GAGE	A. Patriotic song; Yankee ___
D - 2.	OBSERVER	B. Silversmith apprentice turned rebel
T - 3.	JAMES	C. Midwife who tended Johnny's burned hand
K - 4.	LIBERTY	D. Newspaper that printed articles about revolt
V - 5.	PUMPKIN	E. Made Isannah her protegee
B - 6.	JOHNNY	F. Daughter of Liberty
X - 7.	DORCAS	G. Took supplies from Charlestown
F - 8.	BESSIE	H. Said citizens would pay the fiddler: Admiral ___
Y - 9.	LAPHAM	I. Preached more about politics than God
S - 10.	QUINCY	J. Wanted freedom from England
M - 11.	TORIES	K. Leaders in the revolt against England: Sons of ___
L - 12.	CHARLESTOWN	L. General Gage took the cannon and gunpowder from there
E - 13.	LAVINIA	M. They were loyal to England
O - 14.	QUEEN	N. Warned Lexington and Concord of battle
I - 15.	COOPER	O. Popular Boston restaurant: Afric ___
R - 16.	BOSTON	P. Colonists refused to pay tax on it
U - 17.	CONCORD	Q. Owned Boston Observer
J - 18.	WHIGS	R. Setting of the novel
A - 19.	DOODLE	S. Lawyer who defended Johnny for free
P - 20.	TEA	T. Said that a man can stand up
H - 21.	MONTAGUE	U. Town near Lexington
N - 22.	REVERE	V. Gave his musket to Johny
Q - 23.	LORNE	W. Site of first shot of Revolutionary War
C - 24.	HOPPER	X. Ran off with Frizel, Junior
W - 25.	LEXINGTON	Y. Owned silversmith shop

Johnny Tremain Magic Squares 1

Match the definition with the vocabulary word. Put your answers in the magic squares below. When your answers are correct, all columns and rows will add to the same number.

A. LORNE
B. JOHNNY
C. CONCORD
D. GAGE
E. DORCAS
F. QUINCY
G. ADAMS
H. LAVINIA
I. QUEEN
J. WHIGS
K. PUMPKIN
L. NEWMAN
M. GOBLIN
N. DUSTY
O. TEA
P. CHARLESTOWN

1. Silversmith apprentice turned rebel
2. Main speaker at Observer Club meetings
3. Gave his musket to Johny
4. Apprentice who was afraid of Johnny
5. Johnny's horse
6. Hung the lanterns in Christ Church
7. Made Isannah her protege
8. Owned Boston Observer
9. General Gage took the cannon and gunpowder from there
10. Popular Boston restaurant: Afric ___
11. Ran off with Frizel, Junior
12. Took supplies from Charlestown
13. Town near Lexington
14. Lawyer who defended Johnny for free
15. Wanted freedom from England
16. Colonists refused to pay tax on it

A=	B=	C=	D=
E=	F=	G=	H=
I=	J=	K=	L=
M=	N=	O=	P=

Johnny Tremain Magic Squares 1 Answer Key

Match the definition with the vocabulary word. Put your answers in the magic squares below. When your answers are correct, all columns and rows will add to the same number.

A. LORNE
B. JOHNNY
C. CONCORD
D. GAGE
E. DORCAS
F. QUINCY
G. ADAMS
H. LAVINIA
I. QUEEN
J. WHIGS
K. PUMPKIN
L. NEWMAN
M. GOBLIN
N. DUSTY
O. TEA
P. CHARLESTOWN

1. Silversmith apprentice turned rebel
2. Main speaker at Observer Club meetings
3. Gave his musket to Johny
4. Apprentice who was afraid of Johnny
5. Johnny's horse
6. Hung the lanterns in Christ Church
7. Made Isannah her protegee
8. Owned Boston Observer
9. General Gage took the cannon and gunpowder from there
10. Popular Boston restaurant: Afric ___
11. Ran off with Frizel, Junior
12. Took supplies from Charlestown
13. Town near Lexington
14. Lawyer who defended Johnny for free
15. Wanted freedom from England
16. Colonists refused to pay tax on it

A=8	B=1	C=13	D=12
E=11	F=14	G=2	H=7
I=10	J=15	K=3	L=6
M=5	N=4	O=16	P=9

Johnny Tremain Magic Squares 2

Match the definition with the vocabulary word. Put your answers in the magic squares below. When your answers are correct, all columns and rows will add to the same number.

A. FORBES
B. TEA
C. DRAGON
D. LIBERTY
E. MADGE
F. TORIES
G. CONCORD
H. BILLY
I. PUMPKIN
J. CILLA
K. JAMES
L. DOODLE
M. ADAMS
N. BOSTON
O. WHIGS
P. LEXINGTON

1. Wanted freedom from England
2. Lapham daughter intended to marry Johnny
3. Pretended to be drunk to leave the city
4. Author
5. Leaders in the revolt against England: Sons of ____
6. Married a British soldier
7. Said that a man can stand up
8. Setting of the novel
9. They were loyal to England
10. Meeting place for artisans in spy network: Green ___
11. Main speaker at Observer Club meetings
12. Patriotic song; Yankee ___
13. Gave his musket to Johny
14. Site of first shot of Revolutionary War
15. Colonists refusted to pay tax on it
16. Town near Lexington

A=	B=	C=	D=
E=	F=	G=	H=
I=	J=	K=	L=
M=	N=	O=	P=

Johnny Tremain Magic Squares 2 Answer Key

Match the definition with the vocabulary word. Put your answers in the magic squares below. When your answers are correct, all columns and rows will add to the same number.

A. FORBES
B. TEA
C. DRAGON
D. LIBERTY
E. MADGE
F. TORIES
G. CONCORD
H. BILLY
I. PUMPKIN
J. CILLA
K. JAMES
L. DOODLE
M. ADAMS
N. BOSTON
O. WHIGS
P. LEXINGTON

1. Wanted freedom from England
2. Lapham daughter intended to marry Johnny
3. Pretended to be drunk to leave the city
4. Author
5. Leaders in the revolt against England: Sons of ____
6. Married a British soldier
7. Said that a man can stand up
8. Setting of the novel
9. They were loyal to England
10. Meeting place for artisans in spy network: Green ____
11. Main speaker at Observer Club meetings
12. Patriotic song; Yankee ____
13. Gave his musket to Johny
14. Site of first shot of Revolutionary War
15. Colonists refusted to pay tax on it
16. Town near Lexington

A=4	B=15	C=10	D=5
E=6	F=9	G=16	H=3
I=13	J=2	K=7	L=12
M=11	N=8	O=1	P=14

Johnny Tremain Magic Squares 3

Match the definition with the vocabulary word. Put your answers in the magic squares below. When your answers are correct, all columns and rows will add to the same number.

A. LAVINIA
B. DORCAS
C. GOBLIN
D. SMITH
E. TORIES
F. JAMES
G. ADAMS
H. HARBOR
I. HANCOCK
J. TEA
K. LATOUR
L. RAB
M. BILLY
N. CILLA
O. CHARLESTOWN
P. CONCORD

1. Made Isannah her protegee
2. Lapham daughter intended to marry Johnny
3. Colonists refused to pay tax on it
4. They were loyal to England
5. Main speaker at Observer Club meetings
6. First to hear Johnny's story
7. Town near Lexington
8. Johnny's horse
9. General Gage took the cannon and gunpowder from there
10. In charge of British troops at battle in Lexington
11. Where the tea was thrown: Boston ___
12. Johnny's father: Dr. Charles ___
13. Wealthy merchant, ordered sugar basin from Mr. Lapham
14. Said that a man can stand up
15. Ran off with Frizel, Junior
16. Pretended to be drunk to leave the city

A=	B=	C=	D=
E=	F=	G=	H=
I=	J=	K=	L=
M=	N=	O=	P=

Johnny Tremain Magic Squares 3 Answer Key

Match the definition with the vocabulary word. Put your answers in the magic squares below. When your answers are correct, all columns and rows will add to the same number.

A. LAVINIA	E. TORIES	I. HANCOCK	M. BILLY
B. DORCAS	F. JAMES	J. TEA	N. CILLA
C. GOBLIN	G. ADAMS	K. LATOUR	O. CHARLESTOWN
D. SMITH	H. HARBOR	L. RAB	P. CONCORD

1. Made Isannah her protegee
2. Lapham daughter intended to marry Johnny
3. Colonists refused to pay tax on it
4. They were loyal to England
5. Main speaker at Observer Club meetings
6. First to hear Johnny's story
7. Town near Lexington
8. Johnny's horse
9. General Gage took the cannon and gunpowder from there
10. In charge of British troops at battle in Lexington
11. Where the tea was thrown: Boston ___
12. Johnny's father: Dr. Charles ___
13. Wealthy merchant, ordered sugar basin from Mr. Lapham
14. Said that a man can stand up
15. Ran off with Frizel, Junior
16. Pretended to be drunk to leave the city

A=1	B=15	C=8	D=10
E=4	F=14	G=5	H=11
I=13	J=3	K=12	L=6
M=16	N=2	O=9	P=7

Johnny Tremain Magic Squares 4

Match the definition with the vocabulary word. Put your answers in the magic squares below. When your answers are correct, all columns and rows will add to the same number.

A. ISANNAH   E. OBSERVER   I. BILLY   M. HARBOR
B. LIBERTY   F. BOSTON   J. MADGE   N. BESSIE
C. NEWMAN   G. TWEEDIE   K. QUEEN   O. DUSTY
D. JOHNNY   H. CHARLESTOWN   L. CONCORD   P. LYTE

1. Hung the lanterns in Christ Church
2. Married a British soldier
3. Setting of the novel
4. Apprentice who was afraid of Johnny
5. Greedy merchant: Jonathan ___
6. Newspaper that printed articles about revolt
7. Pretended to be drunk to leave the city
8. Silversmith apprentice turned rebel
9. Where the tea was thrown: Boston ___
10. General Gage took the cannon and gunpowder from there
11. Town near Lexington
12. Attracted many because of her frail nature
13. Leaders in the revolt against England: Sons of ___
14. Popular Boston restaurant: Afric ___
15. Silversmith from Baltimore: Percival ___
16. Daughter of Liberty

A=	B=	C=	D=
E=	F=	G=	H=
I=	J=	K=	L=
M=	N=	O=	P=

Johnny Tremain Magic Squares 4 Answer Key

Match the definition with the vocabulary word. Put your answers in the magic squares below. When your answers are correct, all columns and rows will add to the same number.

A. ISANNAH   E. OBSERVER   I. BILLY   M. HARBOR
B. LIBERTY   F. BOSTON   J. MADGE   N. BESSIE
C. NEWMAN   G. TWEEDIE   K. QUEEN   O. DUSTY
D. JOHNNY   H. CHARLESTOWN   L. CONCORD   P. LYTE

1. Hung the lanterns in Christ Church
2. Married a British soldier
3. Setting of the novel
4. Apprentice who was afraid of Johnny
5. Greedy merchant: Jonathan ___
6. Newspaper that printed articles about revolt
7. Pretended to be drunk to leave the city
8. Silversmith apprentice turned rebel
9. Where the tea was thrown: Boston ___
10. General Gage took the cannon and gunpowder from there
11. Town near Lexington
12. Attracted many because of her frail nature
13. Leaders in the revolt against England: Sons of ___
14. Popular Boston restaurant: Afric ___
15. Silversmith from Baltimore: Percival ___
16. Daughter of Liberty

A=12	B=13	C=1	D=8
E=6	F=3	G=15	H=10
I=7	J=2	K=14	L=11
M=9	N=16	O=4	P=5

Johnny Tremain Word Search 1

```
J F P R V C L E X I N G T O N L L N Y
B O T M Y Z O A C D X W H O Y J G L P
X R X Y I C D N P L S L A G R Q L K W
G B Q U I N C Y C H A N N A S I P A P
N E B D A G U V P O A J C H B R E H V
C S X L O V A T L P R M O A D T H S S
G O G D T O D G E P W D C R R U G M S
G N O G A R D R E E A R K B E S S I E
E V B P M C E L I R R D A O O H K T V
E L S P E V T D E X R R A R Z S N H Y
S A E S E R E D F S E P K M Q Y T J P
T V R R B E G D A M N D N C S L W O B
R I V Y W G J C Y E O I D I Z O H H N
A N E T V X R J E N K N T L D R I N T
N I R R W O L U A P I S T L B N G N X
G A T E D N Q M M L E N W A G E S Y F
E F K B X W W U B M T F P Z G G V H T
R Y M I J E P O A B Y T N Y F U H P X
J V X L N Q G J J F L A T O U R E H V
```

Apprentice who was afraid of Johnny (5)
Attracted many because of her frail nature (7)
Author (6)
Colonial army: ___ Men (6)
Colonists refusted to pay tax on it (3)
Daughter of Liberty (6)
First to hear Johnny's story (3)
Gave Johnny a broken crucible (4)
Gave his musket to Johny (7)
Greedy merchant: Jonathan ___ (4)
Hung the lanterns in Christ Church (6)
In charge of British troops at battle in Lexington (5)
Johnny's father: Dr. Charles ___ (6)
Johnny's horse (6)
Lapham daughter intended to marry Johnny (5)
Lawyer who defended Johnny for free (6)
Leaders in the revolt against England: Sons of ___ (7)
Made Isannah her protegee (7)
Main speaker at Observer Club meetings (5)
Married a British soldier (5)
Meeting place for artisans in spy network: Green ___ (6)
Midwife who tended Johnny's burned hand (6)
Newspaper that printed articles about revolt (8)
Owned Boston Observer (5)
Owned silversmith shop (6)
Owner of the colonies (7)
Patriotic song; Yankee ___ (6)
Popular Boston restaurant: Afric ___ (5)
Preached more about politics than God (6)
Pretended to be drunk to leave the city (5)
Ran off with Frizel, Junior (6)
Said citizens would pay the fiddler: Admiral ___ (8)
Said that a man can stand up (5)
Setting of the novel (6)
Silversmith apprentice turned rebel (6)
Silversmith from Baltimore: Percival ___ (7)
Site of first shot of Revolutionary War (9)
Taught Johnny to ride a horse (8)
They were loyal to England (6)
Took supplies from Charlestown (4)
Town near Lexington (7)
Treated Johnny's burned hand (6)
Wanted freedom from England (5)
Warned Lexington and Concord of battle (6)
Wealthy merchant, ordered sugar basin from Mr. Lapham (7)
Where the tea was thrown: Boston ___ (6)

Johnny Tremain Word Search 1 Answer Key

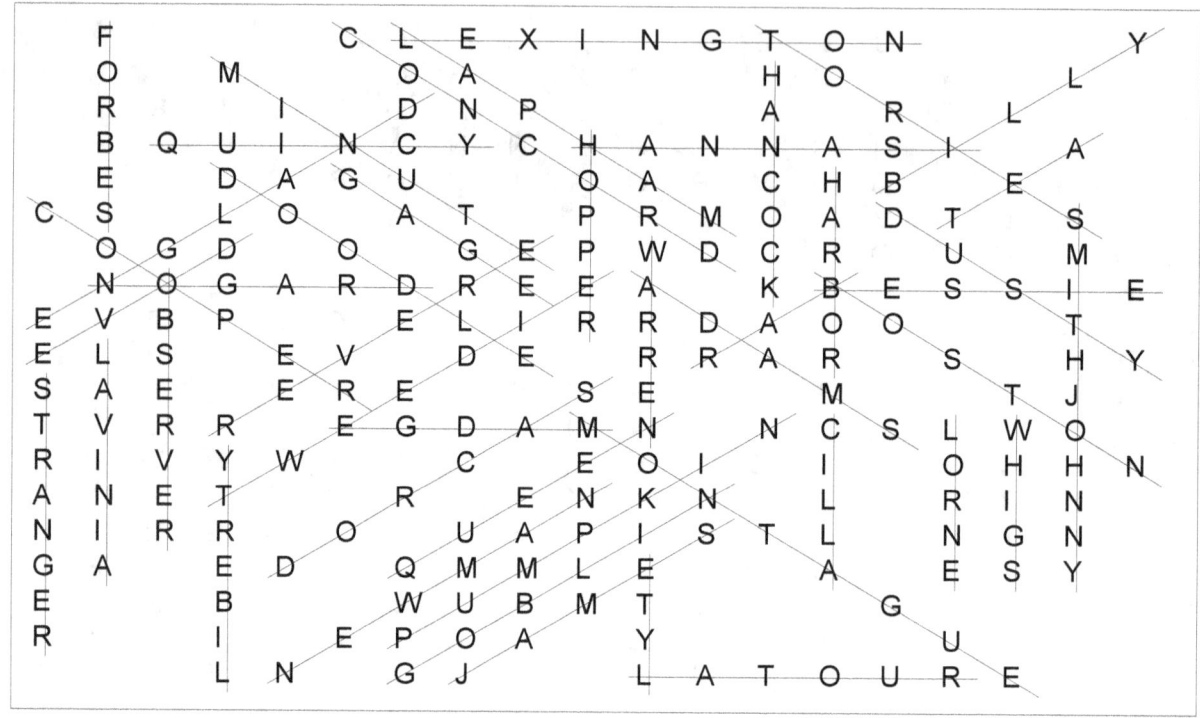

Apprentice who was afraid of Johnny (5)
Attracted many because of her frail nature (7)
Author (6)
Colonial army: ___ Men (6)
Colonists refused to pay tax on it (3)
Daughter of Liberty (6)
First to hear Johnny's story (3)
Gave Johnny a broken crucible (4)
Gave his musket to Johny (7)
Greedy merchant: Jonathan ___ (4)
Hung the lanterns in Christ Church (6)
In charge of British troops at battle in Lexington (5)
Johnny's father: Dr. Charles ___ (6)
Johnny's horse (6)
Lapham daughter intended to marry Johnny (5)
Lawyer who defended Johnny for free (6)
Leaders in the revolt against England: Sons of ___ (7)
Made Isannah her protegee (7)
Main speaker at Observer Club meetings (5)
Married a British soldier (5)
Meeting place for artisans in spy network: Green ___ (6)
Midwife who tended Johnny's burned hand (6)

Newspaper that printed articles about revolt (8)
Owned Boston Observer (5)
Owned silversmith shop (6)
Owner of the colonies (7)
Patriotic song; Yankee ___ (6)
Popular Boston restaurant: Afric ___ (5)
Preached more about politics than God (6)
Pretended to be drunk to leave the city (5)
Ran off with Frizel, Junior (6)
Said citizens would pay the fiddler: Admiral ___ (8)
Said that a man can stand up (5)
Setting of the novel (6)
Silversmith apprentice turned rebel (6)
Silversmith from Baltimore: Percival ___ (7)
Site of first shot of Revolutionary War (9)
Taught Johnny to ride a horse (8)
They were loyal to England (6)
Took supplies from Charlestown (4)
Town near Lexington (7)
Treated Johnny's burned hand (6)
Wanted freedom from England (5)
Warned Lexington and Concord of battle (6)
Wealthy merchant, ordered sugar basin from Mr. Lapham (7)
Where the tea was thrown: Boston ___ (6)

Johnny Tremain Word Search 2

```
M I N U T E Y G D N A L G N E Q W O Z
G O B L I N T M O N T A G U E U V B W
Q U I N C Y R Q R M S D P Q E E L S L
S T R A N G E R C N Y W O C V E Y E M
F D H K V D B N A D E N F O O N T R T
O M L T O R I E S H T W E E D I E V H
R A A L D K L M T Y H O M B L L P E S
B D T B P R A I N I F T Y A O Z E R S
E G O M W D M N G V Q S D J N S Y J C
S E U A A S H S I L V E R S M I T H Y
K P R H P O O W Z G R L A A V S S O J
Q C C P J J P M L E M R G Z B A U B N
W R O A N W P R V F K A O F Q N D I F
H S N L P H E E X J E H N R W N B L S
L F C B X C R H M G S C E C A E L M
H O O B Z I Z B A E G P Z R S H S Y B
J W R G L L K G M R O B R A H J S L Y
Y J D N H L Y A K O Z A W E W Y I F L
T D V M E A J D C T W D H T X X E D J
```

Apprentice who was afraid of Johnny (5)
Attracted many because of her frail nature (7)
Author (6)
Colonial army: ___ Men (6)
Colonists refused to pay tax on it (3)
Daughter of Liberty (6)
First to hear Johnny's story (3)
Gave Johnny a broken crucible (4)
Gave his musket to Johny (7)
General Gage took the cannon and gunpowder from there (11)
Greedy merchant: Jonathan ___ (4)
Hung the lanterns in Christ Church (6)
In charge of British troops at battle in Lexington (5)
Johnny's father: Dr. Charles ___ (6)
Johnny's first occupation (11)
Johnny's horse (6)
Lapham daughter intended to marry Johnny (5)
Lawyer who defended Johnny for free (6)
Leaders in the revolt against England: Sons of ____ (7)
Main speaker at Observer Club meetings (5)
Married a British soldier (5)
Meeting place for artisans in spy network: Green ___ (6)

Midwife who tended Johnny's burned hand (6)
Newspaper that printed articles about revolt (8)
Owned Boston Observer (5)
Owned silversmith shop (6)
Owner of the colonies (7)
Patriotic song; Yankee ___ (6)
Popular Boston restaurant: Afric ___ (5)
Preached more about politics than God (6)
Pretended to be drunk to leave the city (5)
Ran off with Frizel, Junior (6)
Said citizens would pay the fiddler: Admiral ___ (8)
Said that a man can stand up (5)
Setting of the novel (6)
Silversmith apprentice turned rebel (6)
Silversmith from Baltimore: Percival ___ (7)
Taught Johnny to ride a horse (8)
They were loyal to England (6)
Took supplies from Charlestown (4)
Town near Lexington (7)
Treated Johnny's burned hand (6)
Wanted freedom from England (5)
Warned Lexington and Concord of battle (6)
Where the tea was thrown: Boston ___ (6)

Johnny Tremain Word Search 2 Answer Key

Apprentice who was afraid of Johnny (5)
Attracted many because of her frail nature (7)
Author (6)
Colonial army: ___ Men (6)
Colonists refusted to pay tax on it (3)
Daughter of Liberty (6)
First to hear Johnny's story (3)
Gave Johnny a broken crucible (4)
Gave his musket to Johny (7)
General Gage took the cannon and gunpowder from there (11)
Greedy merchant: Jonathan ___ (4)
Hung the lanterns in Christ Church (6)
In charge of British troops at battle in Lexington (5)
Johnny's father: Dr. Charles ___ (6)
Johnny's first occupation (11)
Johnny's horse (6)
Lapham daughter intended to marry Johnny (5)
Lawyer who defended Johnny for free (6)
Leaders in the revolt against England: Sons of ____ (7)
Main speaker at Observer Club meetings (5)
Married a British soldier (5)
Meeting place for artisans in spy network: Green ___ (6)

Midwife who tended Johnny's burned hand (6)
Newspaper that printed articles about revolt (8)
Owned Boston Observer (5)
Owned silversmith shop (6)
Owner of the colonies (7)
Patriotic song; Yankee ___ (6)
Popular Boston restaurant: Afric ___ (5)
Preached more about politics than God (6)
Pretended to be drunk to leave the city (5)
Ran off with Frizel, Junior (6)
Said citizens would pay the fiddler: Admiral ___ (8)
Said that a man can stand up (5)
Setting of the novel (6)
Silversmith apprentice turned rebel (6)
Silversmith from Baltimore: Percival ___ (7)
Taught Johnny to ride a horse (8)
They were loyal to England (6)
Took supplies from Charlestown (4)
Town near Lexington (7)
Treated Johnny's burned hand (6)
Wanted freedom from England (5)
Warned Lexington and Concord of battle (6)
Where the tea was thrown: Boston ___ (6)

Johnny Tremain Word Search 3

```
L D G S P L L R D D X S H N G P B V X T
E V O C B G I P X O R W A L E R H Y N B
X C D O C O R B H K R N N D Q W V S R B
I R W Q D B P P E C E C N P F M M E H G
N Y L Z W L S E B R O F A I N I V A L V
G H R X Y I E T R Z T D S S C E R L N L
T G R T Y N V A N L A Y I T R B C L V L
O F E V O D W E A M G L S E O F S I H F
N B B J P Z E T S Z A O Z R M R M C T S
V J S S D U O L H S G R W B O F I Y I K
C N K E Q U M L G O E N D A N J T E M X
B Z Q M R W S I A M P E R R T M H N S Z
I O C A D V H T N P C P S M A Z D G R F
L D S J H W E D R U H J E D G G R L E R
L P U T B J C R J A T A G R U X O A V R
Y U C S O H D H Y Q N E M M E G B N L G
C M M O T N L G A G W G J Y I S M D I Z
N P Y K O Y F Z T R N G E X S X F M S T
I K T X V P Z W D Q L K R R S P D Y X Q
U I G G P D E R L Z C E V W E D N T Z G
Q N F P M E O R Z O V L S R B N L P X D
X G T R D C K X C F Y S K T H W S T K N
S W F I N W P N C Y R M T O O V P T D Z
S S E O Z B A L B K F L J Y Z W Q Q F D
M L C S R H N C V S W F W S Q B N T Z L
```

ADAMS	DUSTY	LATOUR	QUEEN
BESSIE	ENGLAND	LAVINIA	QUINCY
BILLY	FORBES	LEXINGTON	RAB
BOSTON	GAGE	LIBERTY	REVERE
CHARLESTOWN	GOBLIN	LORNE	SILVERSMITH
CILLA	HANCOCK	LYTE	SMITH
CONCORD	HARBOR	MADGE	STRANGER
COOPER	HOPPER	MINUTE	TEA
DOODLE	ISANNAH	MONTAGUE	TORIES
DORCAS	JAMES	NEWMAN	TWEEDIE
DOVE	JOHNNY	OBSERVER	WARREN
DRAGON	LAPHAM	PUMPKIN	WHIGS

Johnny Tremain Word Search 3 Answer Key

ADAMS	DUSTY	LATOUR	QUEEN
BESSIE	ENGLAND	LAVINIA	QUINCY
BILLY	FORBES	LEXINGTON	RAB
BOSTON	GAGE	LIBERTY	REVERE
CHARLESTOWN	GOBLIN	LORNE	SILVERSMITH
CILLA	HANCOCK	LYTE	SMITH
CONCORD	HARBOR	MADGE	STRANGER
COOPER	HOPPER	MINUTE	TEA
DOODLE	ISANNAH	MONTAGUE	TORIES
DORCAS	JAMES	NEWMAN	TWEEDIE
DOVE	JOHNNY	OBSERVER	WARREN
DRAGON	LAPHAM	PUMPKIN	WHIGS

Johnny Tremain Word Search 4

```
H Z G K F G N W O T S E L R A H C J C G
B S X Q P Q H V H W R G V R N A J F R V
Q B Y Q Y X G K M I Z W Y N M N Q Q X M
B L P T R P H Y C R G P X X Z C W E B M
Y W X W C B A P L F W S W D P O C N R S
H H Y E J O N C Q Z A Y B Z M C O G G B
Q T H E A L N J S Y R H W L L K O L Q H
G V A D M L A C O Q R S O E A Y P A Z P
E O R I E B S Q O H E R V E T J E N A M
R A B E S S I E U R N O T S O B R D H N
E H O L M X L L B E D N U E U V A O O B
V J R I I D R E L P E D Y B R M V R P B
E Z T X O N V G X Y N N T R S X Q C P D
R H M O M A D G E I M O H O R K A A E K
X Y D T N R L N K A N T B F R L T S R Q
Y F T P A D H P H P I G M S L I G Z D F
M R J G K K M P Q M W Y T I E G E A K V
Z O O C C U A K S U W P C O Y R A S G D
Y N N N P L W R R H I S Y T N I V G V E
G M Q T W P E C L T Q N R N N V N E V S
M I R H A V Y S C H B E C I E L W T R X
N N K C L G T S V T B Z V Y F W W Y X M
B U G I V R U X W I M A C S H S M L M V
B T S X K D J E L G L K L S K L W A J Z
R E G N A R T S W Q P B Z D P P V C N C
```

ADAMS	DUSTY	LATOUR	QUEEN
BESSIE	ENGLAND	LAVINIA	QUINCY
BILLY	FORBES	LEXINGTON	RAB
BOSTON	GAGE	LIBERTY	REVERE
CHARLESTOWN	GOBLIN	LORNE	SILVERSMITH
CILLA	HANCOCK	LYTE	SMITH
CONCORD	HARBOR	MADGE	STRANGER
COOPER	HOPPER	MINUTE	TEA
DOODLE	ISANNAH	MONTAGUE	TORIES
DORCAS	JAMES	NEWMAN	TWEEDIE
DOVE	JOHNNY	OBSERVER	WARREN
DRAGON	LAPHAM	PUMPKIN	WHIGS

Johnny Tremain Word Search 4 Answer Key

ADAMS	DUSTY	LATOUR	QUEEN
BESSIE	ENGLAND	LAVINIA	QUINCY
BILLY	FORBES	LEXINGTON	RAB
BOSTON	GAGE	LIBERTY	REVERE
CHARLESTOWN	GOBLIN	LORNE	SILVERSMITH
CILLA	HANCOCK	LYTE	SMITH
CONCORD	HARBOR	MADGE	STRANGER
COOPER	HOPPER	MINUTE	TEA
DOODLE	ISANNAH	MONTAGUE	TORIES
DORCAS	JAMES	NEWMAN	TWEEDIE
DOVE	JOHNNY	OBSERVER	WARREN
DRAGON	LAPHAM	PUMPKIN	WHIGS

Johnny Tremain Crossword 1

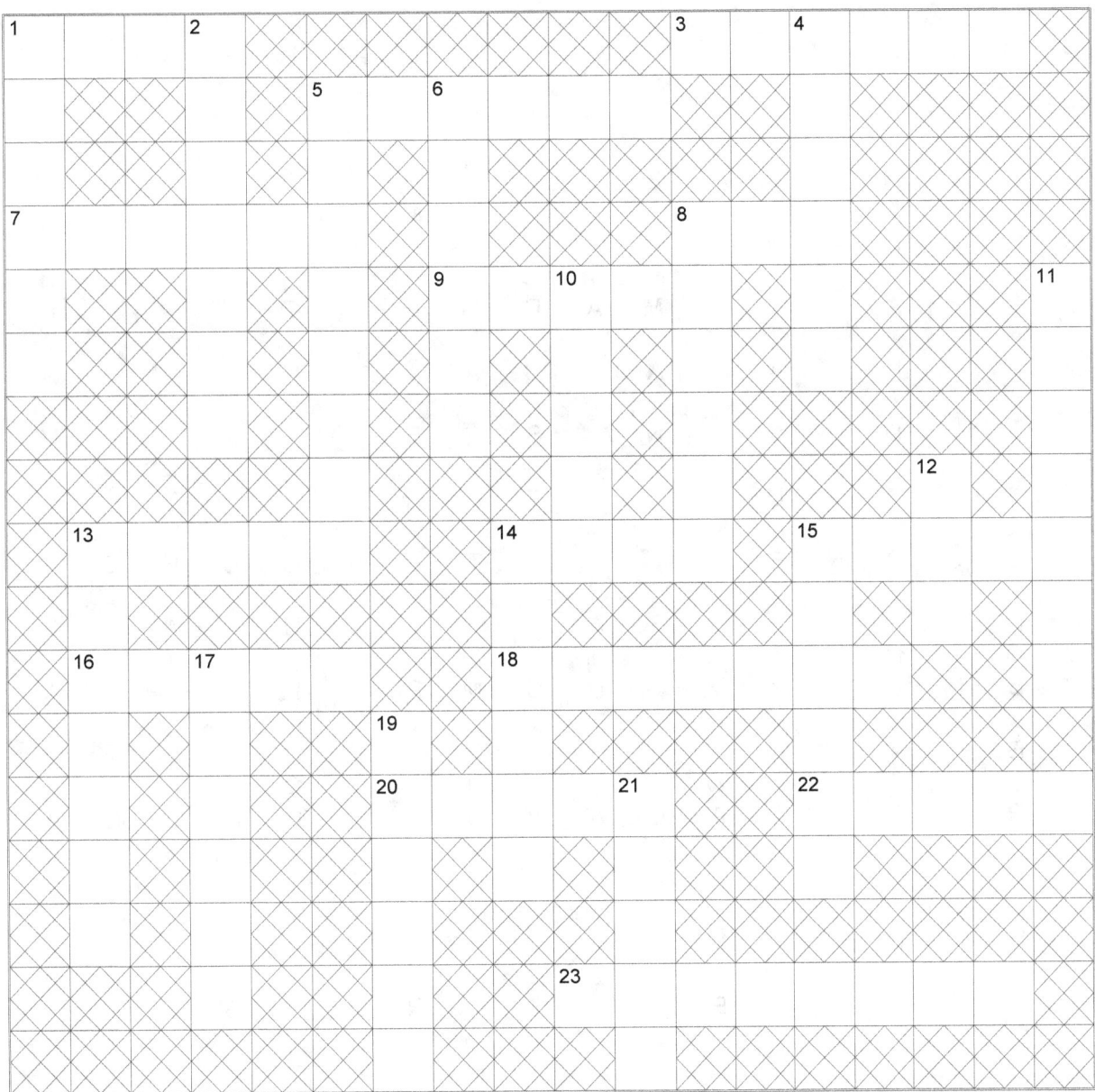

Across
1. Gave Johnny a broken crucible
3. Silversmith apprentice turned rebel
5. Colonial army: ___ Men
7. Johnny's horse
8. First to hear Johnny's story
9. Married a British soldier
13. Owned Boston Observer
14. Greedy merchant: Jonathan ___
15. Popular Boston restaurant: Afric ___
16. Pretended to be drunk to leave the city
18. Gave his musket to Johny
20. Main speaker at Observer Club meetings
22. Lapham daughter intended to marry Johnny
23. Taught Johnny to ride a horse

Down
1. Meeting place for artisans in spy network: Green ___
2. Owner of the colonies
4. Where the tea was thrown: Boston ___
5. Said citizens would pay the fiddler: Admiral ___
6. Hung the lanterns in Christ Church
8. Warned Lexington and Concord of battle
10. Apprentice who was afraid of Johnny
11. Made Isannah her protegee
12. Colonists refusted to pay tax on it
13. Leaders in the revolt against England: Sons of ____
14. Owned silversmith shop
15. Lawyer who defended Johnny for free
17. Johnny's father: Dr. Charles ___
19. Treated Johnny's burned hand
21. In charge of British troops at battle in Lexington

Johnny Tremain Crossword 1 Answer Key

	1 D	O	2 V	E					3 J	O	4 H	N	N	Y
	R		N		5 M	I	6 N	U	T	E		A		
	A		G		O		E					R		
	7 G	O	B	L	I	N		W		8 R	A	B		
	O		A		T		9 M	10 A	D	G	E	O		11 L
	N		N		A		A		N		S		E	V	R			12 T	A
		13 L	O	R	N	E		14 L	Y	T	E		15 Q	U	E	E	N
		I						A					U		A		I
		16 B	17 I	L	L	Y		18 P	U	M	P	K	I	N		A
		E	A				19 W	H				N			
		R	T			20 A	D	A	M	21 S		22 C	I	L	L	A
		T	O			R		M	M			Y			
		Y	U			R			I						
			R			E			23 S	T	R	A	N	G	E	R
							N				H						

Across
1. Gave Johnny a broken crucible
3. Silversmith apprentice turned rebel
5. Colonial army: ___ Men
7. Johnny's horse
8. First to hear Johnny's story
9. Married a British soldier
13. Owned Boston Observer
14. Greedy merchant: Jonathan ___
15. Popular Boston restaurant: Afric ___
16. Pretended to be drunk to leave the city
18. Gave his musket to Johny
20. Main speaker at Observer Club meetings
22. Lapham daughter intended to marry Johnny
23. Taught Johnny to ride a horse

Down
1. Meeting place for artisans in spy network: Green ___
2. Owner of the colonies
4. Where the tea was thrown: Boston ___
5. Said citizens would pay the fiddler: Admiral ___
6. Hung the lanterns in Christ Church
8. Warned Lexington and Concord of battle
10. Apprentice who was afraid of Johnny
11. Made Isannah her protegee
12. Colonists refusted to pay tax on it
13. Leaders in the revolt against England: Sons of ____
14. Owned silversmith shop
15. Lawyer who defended Johnny for free
17. Johnny's father: Dr. Charles ___
19. Treated Johnny's burned hand
21. In charge of British troops at battle in Lexington

Johnny Tremain Crossword 2

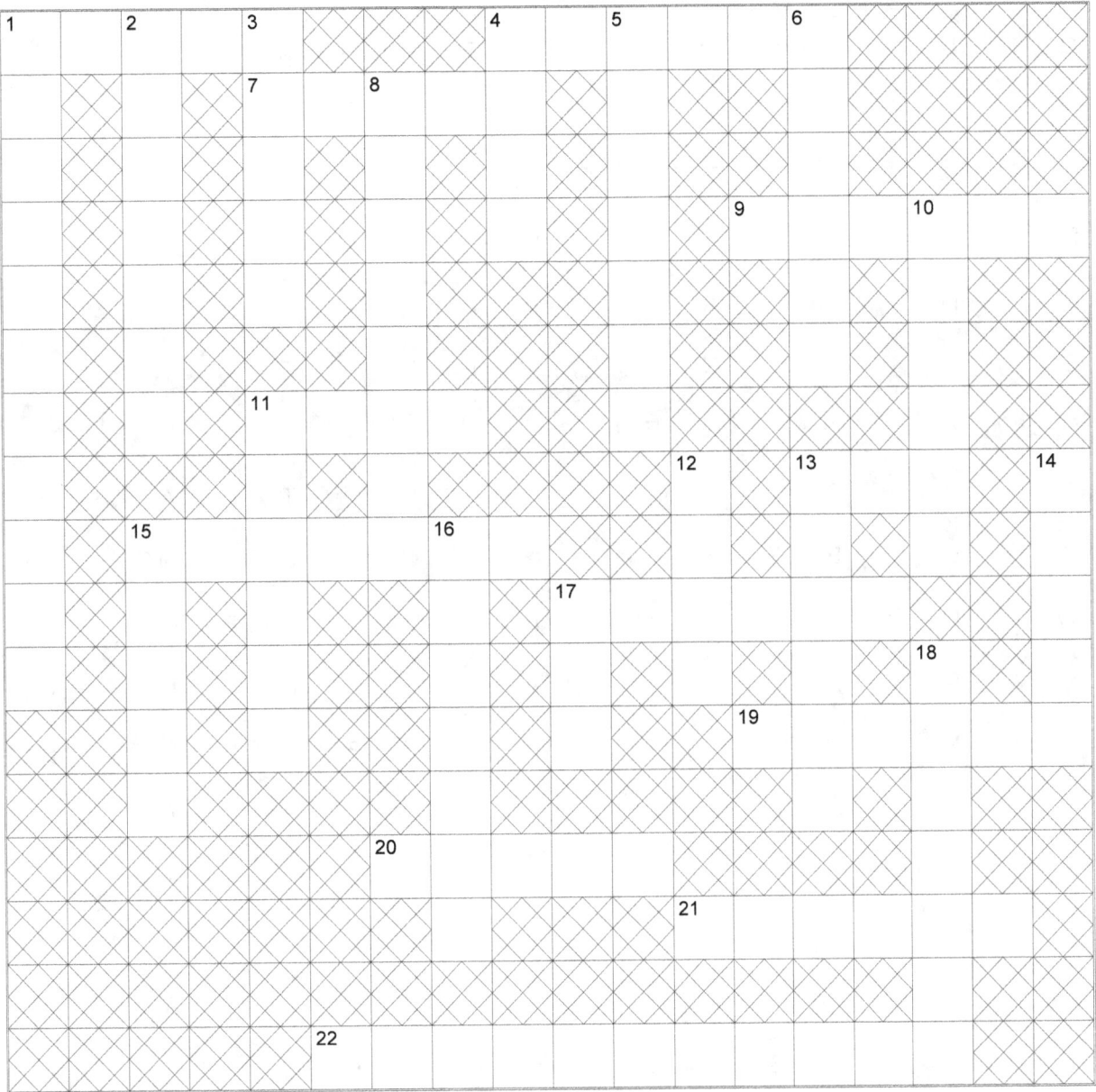

Across
1. Lapham daughter intended to marry Johnny
4. Owned silversmith shop
7. Apprentice who was afraid of Johnny
9. Lawyer who defended Johnny for free
11. Took supplies from Charlestown
13. Colonists refused to pay tax on it
15. Leaders in the revolt against England: Sons of ____
17. Warned Lexington and Concord of battle
19. Daughter of Liberty
20. Pretended to be drunk to leave the city
21. Silversmith apprentice turned rebel
22. Johnny's first occupation

Down
1. General Gage took the cannon and gunpowder from there
2. Made Isannah her protegee
3. Main speaker at Observer Club meetings
4. Greedy merchant: Jonathan ___
5. Gave his musket to Johny
6. Colonial army: ___ Men
8. Taught Johnny to ride a horse
10. Hung the lanterns in Christ Church
11. Johnny's horse
12. Gave Johnny a broken crucible
13. They were loyal to England
14. Married a British soldier
15. Owned Boston Observer
16. Silversmith from Baltimore: Percival ___
17. First to hear Johnny's story
18. Attracted many because of her frail nature

Johnny Tremain Crossword 2 Answer Key

	1 C	2 I	3 L	L	A		4 L	5 A	P	H	A	6 M		
	H		A	7 D	8 U	S	T	Y		5 U		I		
	A		V	A		T	T		M			N		
	R		I	M	R		E		P		9 Q	U	I	10 N	C	Y
	L		N	S	A				K		U		T		E	
	E		I		N				I		N		T		W	
	S		A	11 G	A	G	E		N		C		E		M	
	T			O	E					12 D	13 T	E	A		14 M
	O		15 L	I	B	E	R	T	Y			O	O		N		A
	W		O	L			W	17 R	E	V	E	R	E			D
	N		R				E	A			E		I	18 I		G
			N	N			E	B			19 B	E	S	S	I	E
			E				D						S	A		
					20 B	I	L	L	Y					N		
					E			21 J	O	H	N	N	Y			
														A		
				22 S	I	L	V	E	R	S	M	I	T	H		

Across
1. Lapham daughter intended to marry Johnny
4. Owned silversmith shop
7. Apprentice who was afraid of Johnny
9. Lawyer who defended Johnny for free
11. Took supplies from Charlestown
13. Colonists refused to pay tax on it
15. Leaders in the revolt against England: Sons of ____
17. Warned Lexington and Concord of battle
19. Daughter of Liberty
20. Pretended to be drunk to leave the city
21. Silversmith apprentice turned rebel
22. Johnny's first occupation

Down
1. General Gage took the cannon and gunpowder from there
2. Made Isannah her protegee
3. Main speaker at Observer Club meetings
4. Greedy merchant: Jonathan ___
5. Gave his musket to Johny
6. Colonial army: ___ Men
8. Taught Johnny to ride a horse
10. Hung the lanterns in Christ Church
11. Johnny's horse
12. Gave Johnny a broken crucible
13. They were loyal to England
14. Married a British soldier
15. Owned Boston Observer
16. Silversmith from Baltimore: Percival ___
17. First to hear Johnny's story
18. Attracted many because of her frail nature

Johnny Tremain Crossword 3

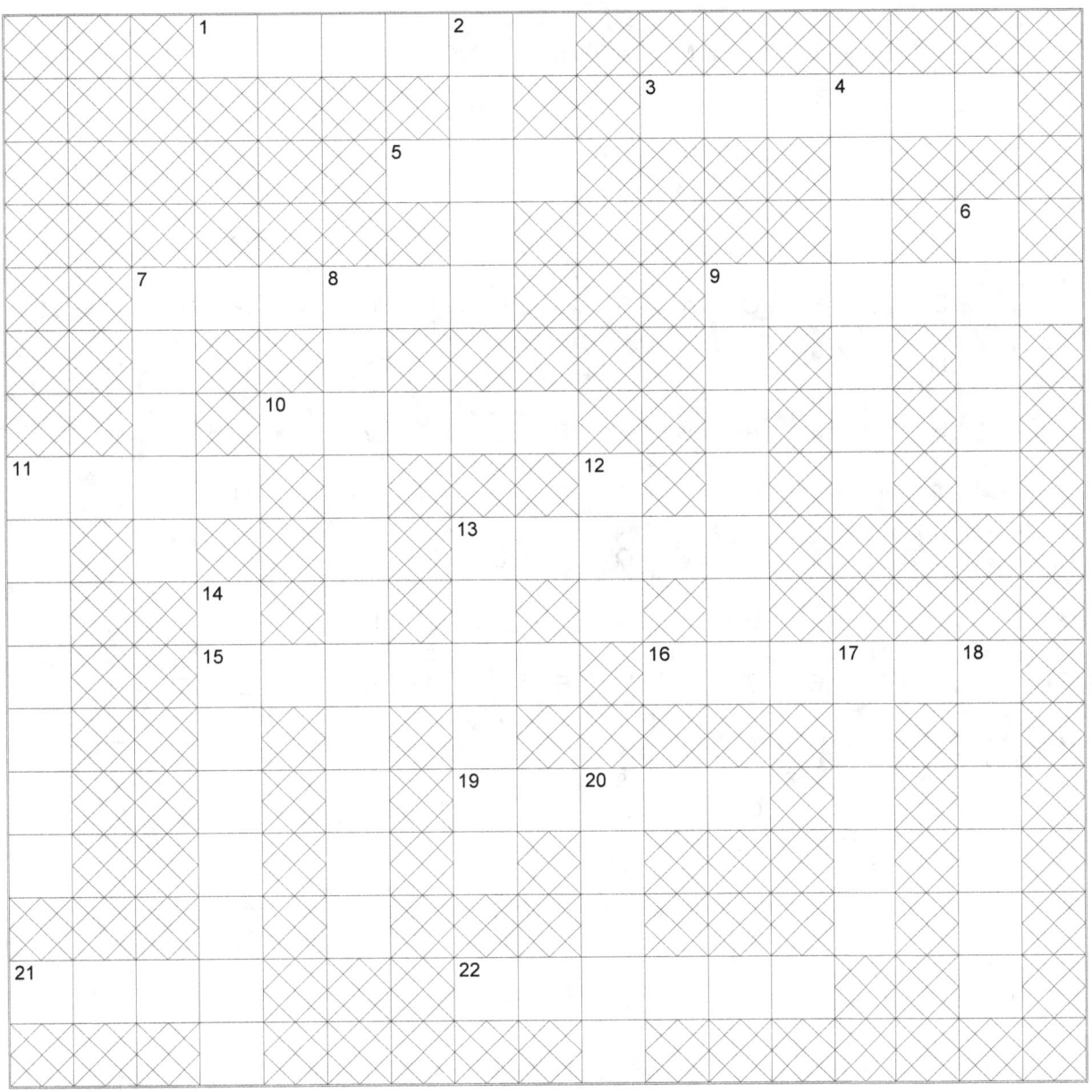

Across
1. Hung the lanterns in Christ Church
3. Midwife who tended Johnny's burned hand
5. First to hear Johnny's story
7. Ran off with Frizel, Junior
9. Owned silversmith shop
10. Said that a man can stand up
11. Greedy merchant: Jonathan ___
13. Popular Boston restaurant: Afric ___
15. Daughter of Liberty
16. Where the tea was thrown: Boston ___
19. Lapham daughter intended to marry Johnny
21. Gave Johnny a broken crucible
22. Colonial army: ___ Men

Down
2. Main speaker at Observer Club meetings
4. Gave his musket to Johny
6. Married a British soldier
7. Apprentice who was afraid of Johnny
8. General Gage took the cannon and gunpowder from there
9. Made Isannah her protegee
11. Leaders in the revolt against England: Sons of ___
12. Colonists refused to pay tax on it
13. Lawyer who defended Johnny for free
14. Newspaper that printed articles about revolt
17. Pretended to be drunk to leave the city
18. Warned Lexington and Concord of battle
20. Owned Boston Observer

Johnny Tremain Crossword 3 Answer Key

			¹N	E	W	²M	A	N					
						A				³H	O	⁴P	P	E	R
					⁵R	A	B					U			
						M						M			⁶M
		⁷D	O	⁸C	A	S			⁹L	A	P	H	A	M
		U		H					A		K			D
		S		¹⁰J	A	M	E	S		V		I			G
¹¹L	Y	T	E	R			¹²T		I		N			E
I		Y		L		¹³Q	U	E	E	N			
B		¹⁴O		E		U		A		I			
E		¹⁵B	E	S	S	I	E		¹⁶H	A	¹⁷R	B	O	¹⁸R
R		S		T		N					I			E
T		E		O		¹⁹C	²⁰L	I	L	L	A			V
Y		R		W		Y		O		L				E
		V		N				R		Y				R
²¹D	O	V	E			²²M	I	N	U	T	E			E
		R						E						

Across
1. Hung the lanterns in Christ Church
3. Midwife who tended Johnny's burned hand
5. First to hear Johnny's story
7. Ran off with Frizel, Junior
9. Owned silversmith shop
10. Said that a man can stand up
11. Greedy merchant: Jonathan ___
13. Popular Boston restaurant: Afric ___
15. Daughter of Liberty
16. Where the tea was thrown: Boston ___
19. Lapham daughter intended to marry Johnny
21. Gave Johnny a broken crucible
22. Colonial army: ___ Men

Down
2. Main speaker at Observer Club meetings
4. Gave his musket to Johny
6. Married a British soldier
7. Apprentice who was afraid of Johnny
8. General Gage took the cannon and gunpowder from there
9. Made Isannah her protegee
11. Leaders in the revolt against England: Sons of ___
12. Colonists refusted to pay tax on it
13. Lawyer who defended Johnny for free
14. Newspaper that printed articles about revolt
17. Pretended to be drunk to leave the city
18. Warned Lexington and Concord of battle
20. Owned Boston Observer

Johnny Tremain Crossword 4

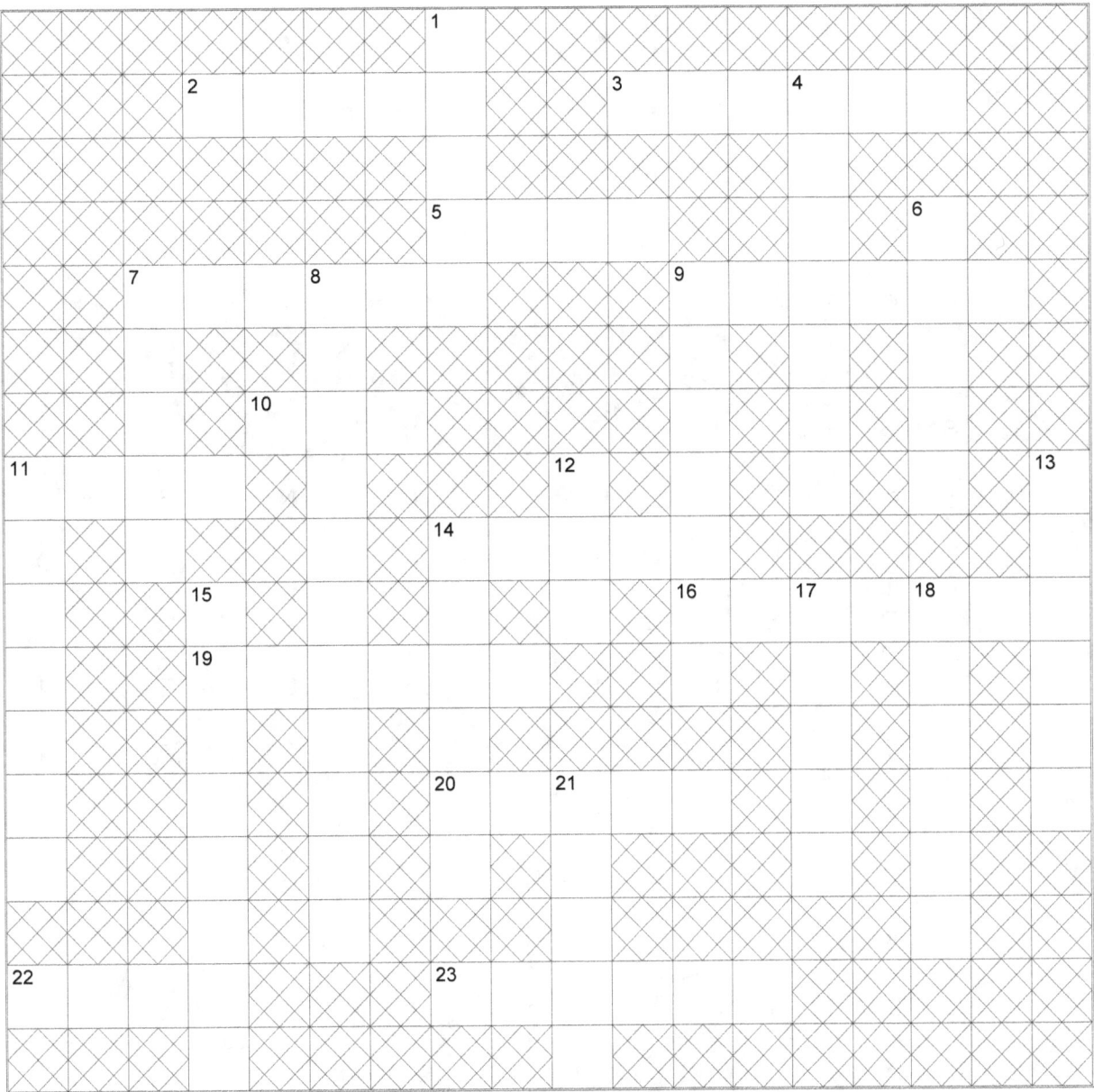

Across
2. In charge of British troops at battle in Lexington
3. Midwife who tended Johnny's burned hand
5. Took supplies from Charlestown
7. Ran off with Frizel, Junior
9. Owned silversmith shop
10. First to hear Johnny's story
11. Greedy merchant: Jonathan ___
14. Popular Boston restaurant: Afric ___
16. Attracted many because of her frail nature
19. Daughter of Liberty
20. Lapham daughter intended to marry Johnny
22. Gave Johnny a broken crucible
23. Colonial army: ___ Men

Down
1. Wanted freedom from England
4. Gave his musket to Johny
6. Married a British soldier
7. Apprentice who was afraid of Johnny
8. General Gage took the cannon and gunpowder from there
9. Made Isannah her protegee
11. Leaders in the revolt against England: Sons of ____
12. Colonists refused to pay tax on it
13. Silversmith apprentice turned rebel
14. Lawyer who defended Johnny for free
15. Newspaper that printed articles about revolt
17. Main speaker at Observer Club meetings
18. Hung the lanterns in Christ Church
21. Owned Boston Observer

Johnny Tremain Crossword 4 Answer Key

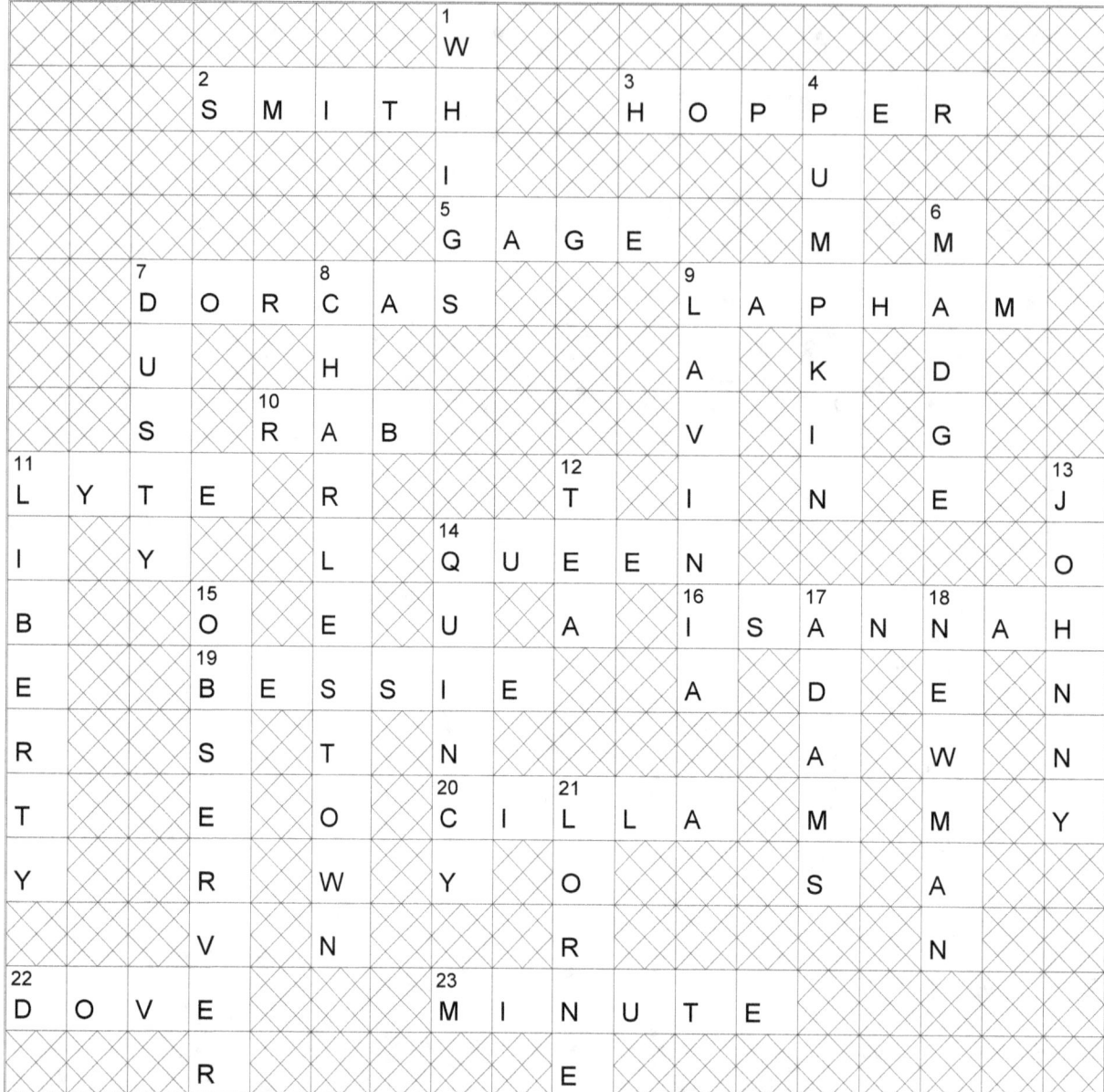

Across
2. In charge of British troops at battle in Lexington
3. Midwife who tended Johnny's burned hand
5. Took supplies from Charlestown
7. Ran off with Frizel, Junior
9. Owned silversmith shop
10. First to hear Johnny's story
11. Greedy merchant: Jonathan ___
14. Popular Boston restaurant: Afric ___
16. Attracted many because of her frail nature
19. Daughter of Liberty
20. Lapham daughter intended to marry Johnny
22. Gave Johnny a broken crucible
23. Colonial army: ___ Men

Down
1. Wanted freedom from England
4. Gave his musket to Johny
6. Married a British soldier
7. Apprentice who was afraid of Johnny
8. General Gage took the cannon and gunpowder from there
9. Made Isannah her protegee
11. Leaders in the revolt against England: Sons of ____
12. Colonists refused to pay tax on it
13. Silversmith apprentice turned rebel
14. Lawyer who defended Johnny for free
15. Newspaper that printed articles about revolt
17. Main speaker at Observer Club meetings
18. Hung the lanterns in Christ Church
21. Owned Boston Observer

Johnny Tremain

LYTE	JOHNNY	HANCOCK	REVERE	CILLA
QUINCY	ISANNAH	SILVERSMITH	DRAGON	COOPER
GOBLIN	CONCORD	FREE SPACE	DORCAS	TEA
DUSTY	DOODLE	WHIGS	LIBERTY	LAVINIA
MINUTE	RAB	BILLY	WARREN	ENGLAND

Johnny Tremain

JAMES	LATOUR	GAGE	HOPPER	SMITH
TWEEDIE	DOVE	FORBES	STRANGER	MADGE
HARBOR	NEWMAN	FREE SPACE	CHARLESTOWN	BESSIE
BOSTON	TORIES	OBSERVER	PUMPKIN	LEXINGTON
LORNE	LAPHAM	ADAMS	ENGLAND	WARREN

Johnny Tremain

WHIGS	OBSERVER	BOSTON	HANCOCK	CHARLESTOWN
TORIES	ISANNAH	TWEEDIE	DORCAS	LAVINIA
JOHNNY	CONCORD	FREE SPACE	GOBLIN	GAGE
SILVERSMITH	TEA	QUINCY	HOPPER	REVERE
NEWMAN	BESSIE	MONTAGUE	FORBES	CILLA

Johnny Tremain

LATOUR	DOVE	LYTE	QUEEN	STRANGER
MADGE	ADAMS	HARBOR	COOPER	DUSTY
LIBERTY	BILLY	FREE SPACE	DRAGON	LAPHAM
JAMES	WARREN	LEXINGTON	SMITH	MINUTE
LORNE	DOODLE	ENGLAND	CILLA	FORBES

Johnny Tremain

CHARLESTOWN	ISANNAH	LAPHAM	COOPER	DOODLE
TWEEDIE	GOBLIN	LYTE	WHIGS	STRANGER
TEA	SILVERSMITH	FREE SPACE	SMITH	MADGE
QUINCY	MINUTE	JOHNNY	BOSTON	GAGE
NEWMAN	LEXINGTON	ADAMS	TORIES	HARBOR

Johnny Tremain

MONTAGUE	CILLA	RAB	DRAGON	OBSERVER
HANCOCK	LORNE	LIBERTY	CONCORD	ENGLAND
FORBES	QUEEN	FREE SPACE	LAVINIA	LATOUR
PUMPKIN	BILLY	BESSIE	DUSTY	HOPPER
DOVE	REVERE	DORCAS	HARBOR	TORIES

Johnny Tremain

MADGE	STRANGER	WARREN	ENGLAND	GAGE
MINUTE	GOBLIN	PUMPKIN	QUEEN	TEA
DUSTY	DOODLE	FREE SPACE	HARBOR	QUINCY
BILLY	LATOUR	CHARLESTOWN	LAPHAM	JOHNNY
REVERE	LORNE	OBSERVER	LAVINIA	CILLA

Johnny Tremain

ISANNAH	DRAGON	HANCOCK	DORCAS	SMITH
CONCORD	LYTE	LIBERTY	COOPER	LEXINGTON
BESSIE	TWEEDIE	FREE SPACE	DOVE	RAB
ADAMS	NEWMAN	MONTAGUE	TORIES	SILVERSMITH
HOPPER	JAMES	WHIGS	CILLA	LAVINIA

Johnny Tremain

QUINCY	HANCOCK	WARREN	LYTE	TWEEDIE
JAMES	GAGE	ENGLAND	NEWMAN	CILLA
QUEEN	BESSIE	FREE SPACE	DOODLE	FORBES
WHIGS	TEA	GOBLIN	LATOUR	COOPER
TORIES	CONCORD	SILVERSMITH	BOSTON	DORCAS

Johnny Tremain

BILLY	SMITH	LEXINGTON	MINUTE	LAVINIA
HOPPER	LAPHAM	LIBERTY	PUMPKIN	STRANGER
LORNE	ISANNAH	FREE SPACE	HARBOR	RAB
DOVE	JOHNNY	DRAGON	ADAMS	MONTAGUE
OBSERVER	REVERE	DUSTY	DORCAS	BOSTON

Johnny Tremain

QUINCY	BOSTON	ISANNAH	TORIES	TEA
DUSTY	STRANGER	WARREN	ENGLAND	SMITH
MADGE	CILLA	FREE SPACE	WHIGS	DORCAS
MINUTE	CHARLESTOWN	REVERE	COOPER	ADAMS
DOVE	LORNE	LIBERTY	SILVERSMITH	LYTE

Johnny Tremain

HOPPER	LAPHAM	BESSIE	JOHNNY	DOODLE
LEXINGTON	QUEEN	FORBES	DRAGON	JAMES
HARBOR	CONCORD	FREE SPACE	RAB	LAVINIA
LATOUR	PUMPKIN	BILLY	GAGE	GOBLIN
NEWMAN	HANCOCK	TWEEDIE	LYTE	SILVERSMITH

Johnny Tremain

LYTE	CHARLESTOWN	LIBERTY	FORBES	TORIES
LATOUR	MONTAGUE	OBSERVER	DOVE	WARREN
COOPER	BESSIE	FREE SPACE	GOBLIN	TWEEDIE
ISANNAH	DORCAS	REVERE	BOSTON	RAB
MADGE	QUINCY	CILLA	BILLY	LEXINGTON

Johnny Tremain

HANCOCK	ADAMS	HOPPER	TEA	DOODLE
LAVINIA	SILVERSMITH	JOHNNY	CONCORD	QUEEN
WHIGS	DUSTY	FREE SPACE	LAPHAM	MINUTE
PUMPKIN	NEWMAN	ENGLAND	HARBOR	STRANGER
SMITH	GAGE	DRAGON	LEXINGTON	BILLY

Johnny Tremain

DOVE	WARREN	QUEEN	QUINCY	MADGE
LAVINIA	BOSTON	SMITH	CONCORD	COOPER
GOBLIN	HARBOR	FREE SPACE	BESSIE	WHIGS
DOODLE	GAGE	JOHNNY	HANCOCK	FORBES
CILLA	OBSERVER	LYTE	LORNE	REVERE

Johnny Tremain

TORIES	ENGLAND	TWEEDIE	NEWMAN	CHARLESTOWN
MONTAGUE	RAB	HOPPER	DUSTY	STRANGER
BILLY	LAPHAM	FREE SPACE	LIBERTY	TEA
ISANNAH	LEXINGTON	ADAMS	MINUTE	DRAGON
PUMPKIN	DORCAS	JAMES	REVERE	LORNE

Johnny Tremain

LYTE	HANCOCK	CHARLESTOWN	DRAGON	DORCAS
MINUTE	LEXINGTON	DOODLE	NEWMAN	PUMPKIN
LIBERTY	STRANGER	FREE SPACE	QUEEN	JAMES
GOBLIN	ISANNAH	TORIES	ADAMS	LATOUR
OBSERVER	MADGE	COOPER	DUSTY	REVERE

Johnny Tremain

WARREN	ENGLAND	CILLA	RAB	HOPPER
FORBES	TWEEDIE	GAGE	LORNE	JOHNNY
DOVE	MONTAGUE	FREE SPACE	TEA	WHIGS
HARBOR	CONCORD	LAPHAM	BOSTON	BILLY
QUINCY	SILVERSMITH	SMITH	REVERE	DUSTY

Johnny Tremain

LYTE	TORIES	CILLA	TWEEDIE	GAGE
ENGLAND	DRAGON	QUINCY	ISANNAH	MADGE
WARREN	LAPHAM	FREE SPACE	COOPER	REVERE
DORCAS	JOHNNY	LAVINIA	MINUTE	DOODLE
WHIGS	DUSTY	LIBERTY	JAMES	GOBLIN

Johnny Tremain

SMITH	CHARLESTOWN	SILVERSMITH	STRANGER	BILLY
PUMPKIN	HANCOCK	TEA	LATOUR	DOVE
BESSIE	LEXINGTON	FREE SPACE	MONTAGUE	FORBES
ADAMS	QUEEN	BOSTON	HARBOR	RAB
OBSERVER	CONCORD	HOPPER	GOBLIN	JAMES

Johnny Tremain

WARREN	ENGLAND	SILVERSMITH	DOVE	GAGE
LAPHAM	TWEEDIE	LORNE	MINUTE	BESSIE
BOSTON	DORCAS	FREE SPACE	MADGE	HOPPER
JAMES	LEXINGTON	GOBLIN	MONTAGUE	HARBOR
WHIGS	COOPER	LIBERTY	REVERE	HANCOCK

Johnny Tremain

ISANNAH	LYTE	DRAGON	DOODLE	JOHNNY
NEWMAN	QUEEN	SMITH	CILLA	PUMPKIN
TORIES	FORBES	FREE SPACE	STRANGER	ADAMS
CHARLESTOWN	BILLY	DUSTY	LATOUR	QUINCY
LAVINIA	OBSERVER	TEA	HANCOCK	REVERE

Johnny Tremain

LEXINGTON	MADGE	OBSERVER	ISANNAH	DORCAS
DUSTY	MINUTE	REVERE	SMITH	DRAGON
CHARLESTOWN	TWEEDIE	FREE SPACE	BOSTON	BILLY
QUINCY	WHIGS	LAVINIA	LYTE	LATOUR
HOPPER	HARBOR	JAMES	HANCOCK	BESSIE

Johnny Tremain

JOHNNY	STRANGER	LAPHAM	SILVERSMITH	DOVE
WARREN	QUEEN	TEA	ENGLAND	GOBLIN
GAGE	LIBERTY	FREE SPACE	COOPER	NEWMAN
RAB	CILLA	ADAMS	LORNE	FORBES
DOODLE	PUMPKIN	TORIES	BESSIE	HANCOCK

Johnny Tremain

TORIES	LAPHAM	DRAGON	CILLA	HARBOR
SILVERSMITH	GAGE	QUINCY	OBSERVER	DOODLE
LAVINIA	TEA	FREE SPACE	HOPPER	WHIGS
LATOUR	MONTAGUE	DORCAS	WARREN	DUSTY
NEWMAN	MINUTE	LIBERTY	GOBLIN	BILLY

Johnny Tremain

CHARLESTOWN	CONCORD	ENGLAND	PUMPKIN	LORNE
LEXINGTON	MADGE	STRANGER	ISANNAH	COOPER
ADAMS	FORBES	FREE SPACE	QUEEN	HANCOCK
BESSIE	SMITH	LYTE	REVERE	JAMES
DOVE	JOHNNY	TWEEDIE	BILLY	GOBLIN

Johnny Tremain

JOHNNY	COOPER	DUSTY	BILLY	NEWMAN
LORNE	MADGE	WHIGS	CONCORD	LATOUR
TEA	STRANGER	FREE SPACE	QUINCY	HOPPER
DOODLE	DRAGON	BOSTON	MONTAGUE	RAB
BESSIE	LIBERTY	MINUTE	DORCAS	WARREN

Johnny Tremain

DOVE	CILLA	HANCOCK	HARBOR	GOBLIN
SMITH	ISANNAH	CHARLESTOWN	TORIES	TWEEDIE
JAMES	QUEEN	FREE SPACE	OBSERVER	LAPHAM
SILVERSMITH	GAGE	ADAMS	ENGLAND	LEXINGTON
LYTE	PUMPKIN	REVERE	WARREN	DORCAS

Johnny Tremain

DOVE	ISANNAH	LIBERTY	SMITH	BESSIE
CILLA	HARBOR	STRANGER	MADGE	DORCAS
HANCOCK	DOODLE	FREE SPACE	WHIGS	DUSTY
NEWMAN	TEA	BOSTON	CONCORD	LYTE
MONTAGUE	GAGE	GOBLIN	HOPPER	DRAGON

Johnny Tremain

ADAMS	BILLY	WARREN	LORNE	LAVINIA
MINUTE	RAB	OBSERVER	QUINCY	SILVERSMITH
PUMPKIN	TORIES	FREE SPACE	TWEEDIE	COOPER
QUEEN	ENGLAND	FORBES	LAPHAM	JOHNNY
JAMES	REVERE	LEXINGTON	DRAGON	HOPPER

Johnny Tremain

HOPPER	DORCAS	BESSIE	REVERE	DUSTY
BOSTON	DOVE	LORNE	CHARLESTOWN	WARREN
MINUTE	ADAMS	FREE SPACE	ENGLAND	QUINCY
LATOUR	JOHNNY	LIBERTY	DOODLE	RAB
CILLA	TWEEDIE	DRAGON	QUEEN	BILLY

Johnny Tremain

LAPHAM	OBSERVER	LYTE	SMITH	WHIGS
GAGE	JAMES	CONCORD	GOBLIN	PUMPKIN
SILVERSMITH	HARBOR	FREE SPACE	TEA	HANCOCK
TORIES	FORBES	LAVINIA	LEXINGTON	ISANNAH
MADGE	NEWMAN	COOPER	BILLY	QUEEN

Johnny Tremain Vocabulary Word List

No.	Word	Clue/Definition
1.	ABATED	Reduced in amount
2.	APOPLECTIC	Having loss of muscular control & sensation
3.	APPARITION	Ghost
4.	APPRENTICES	Those who work in return for instruction
5.	ARDENT	Passionate; displaying a strong enthusiasm
6.	AROUSE	Awaken or excite
7.	ARROGANTLY	Boastfully
8.	ARSENAL	A supply of weapons
9.	AVERTED	Turned away
10.	BARTERING	Trading goods or services without money
11.	BELFRY	Bell tower
12.	BELLIGERENT	Eager to fight; hostile
13.	BERATED	Rebuked; scolded; put down
14.	CANNY	Careful and shrewd
15.	CIVIL	Relating to a citizen
16.	CLAMOR	Uproar
17.	COMPASSIONATE	Sympathetic
18.	CONCOCTION	Food or beverage made of mixed ingredients
19.	CORDIALLY	Sincerely; warmly
20.	CRUCIBLE	Porcelain dish used for melting silver
21.	CULTIVATE	To nurture
22.	DEMEANOR	The way in which a person behaves
23.	DETESTED	Hated
24.	DIFFIDENTLY	Shyly; timidly
25.	DILAPIDATED	Broken-down
26.	DILIGENTLY	In a hard-working manner
27.	DISCONSOLATELY	Cheerlessly; gloomily
28.	DISPERSE	To scatter in different directions
29.	ENIGMATICAL	Puzzling
30.	ETHEREAL	Airy; fragile
31.	FATUOUS	Unconsciously foolish
32.	FLACCID	Lacking vigor or energy
33.	GLOATING	Expressing great pleasure or self-satisfaction
34.	GRIEVANCES	Reasons for protest; complaints
35.	HERETIC	Misbeliever; one who holds controversial opinions
36.	IMPERCEPTIBLY	Not noticeably
37.	INCAPACITY	Inadequate strength or ability
38.	INDENTURE	Unpaid service to another
39.	INDOLENT	Habitually lazy
40.	INSTIGATED	Started; initiated
41.	INSURRECTION	An open revolt
42.	INUNDATED	Overwhelmed; swamped
43.	INVINCIBLE	Unconquerable
44.	LAGGARD	Hanging back or falling behind
45.	LAMENTABLE	Regrettable
46.	LENIENT	Merciful; indulgent
47.	LOITERING	Standing idly about; lingering aimlessly
48.	LUCID	Easily understood; intelligible
49.	MARTIAL	Relating to war

Copyrighted

Johnny Tremain Vocabulary Word List

No.	Word	Clue/Definition
50.	MUNDANE	Ordinary; boring
51.	NONCHALANT	Unconcerned or indifferent
52.	ORATORY	Relating to public speaking
53.	PARASITIC	Taking advantage of others without useful return
54.	PAROXYSM	A spasm or fit
55.	PERIL	Danger
56.	PIETY	Reverence
57.	PIQUED	Felt wounded pride
58.	PLACATE	To appease; make concessions
59.	POULTICE	Dressing for a wound or injury
60.	PRETENSE	A false action intended to deceive
61.	PRODIGIOUSLY	In an impressively great way
62.	PROMENADE	A public place for walking
63.	PROTEGEE	One whose welfare is promoted by another
64.	PROTUBERANT	Swelling outward; bulging
65.	PUNCTILIOUS	Precise; scrupulous
66.	QUALMS	Uneasy feelings
67.	REPENTANCE	Remorse or contrition
68.	REPROVED	Found fault with
69.	REVERTED	Returned to a former condition
70.	SEDITIOUS	Rebellious
71.	SOLITARY	Alone
72.	STRIFE	A struggle or fight
73.	SUBDUED	Brought under control; quieted
74.	SURFEITED	Saturated; overfilled
75.	TEDIOUSLY	Slowly; in a boring manner
76.	TENTATIVELY	Uncertainly; hesitantly
77.	TREASON	Betrayal of one's country
78.	TRIVIAL	Of little significance or value
79.	TURBULENT	Violently agitated or disturbed
80.	TYRANNY	Unjust use of absolute power
81.	WARY	On guard; watchful
82.	WAVERED	Showed indecision

Copyrighted

Johnny Tremain Vocabulary Fill In The Blank 1

1. Reduced in amount
2. Unconquerable
3. Uproar
4. A false action intended to deceive
5. Alone
6. Having loss of muscular control & sensation
7. To nurture
8. Sincerely; warmly
9. Boastfully
10. Shyly; timidly
11. Merciful; indulgent
12. In an impressively great way
13. Hanging back or falling behind
14. Hated
15. Uncertainly; hesitantly
16. Airy; fragile
17. A public place for walking
18. Puzzling
19. Food or beverage made of mixed ingredients
20. To appease; make concessions

Johnny Tremain Vocabulary Fill In The Blank 1 Answer Key

ABATED	1. Reduced in amount
INVINCIBLE	2. Unconquerable
CLAMOR	3. Uproar
PRETENSE	4. A false action intended to deceive
SOLITARY	5. Alone
APOPLECTIC	6. Having loss of muscular control & sensation
CULTIVATE	7. To nurture
CORDIALLY	8. Sincerely; warmly
ARROGANTLY	9. Boastfully
DIFFIDENTLY	10. Shyly; timidly
LENIENT	11. Merciful; indulgent
PRODIGIOUSLY	12. In an impressively great way
LAGGARD	13. Hanging back or falling behind
DETESTED	14. Hated
TENTATIVELY	15. Uncertainly; hesitantly
ETHEREAL	16. Airy; fragile
PROMENADE	17. A public place for walking
ENIGMATICAL	18. Puzzling
CONCOCTION	19. Food or beverage made of mixed ingredients
PLACATE	20. To appease; make concessions

Johnny Tremain Vocabulary Fill In The Blank 2

_____ 1. Started; initiated

_____ 2. Swelling outward; bulging

_____ 3. Broken-down

_____ 4. Felt wounded pride

_____ 5. Careful and shrewd

_____ 6. Passionate; displaying a strong enthusiasm

_____ 7. Returned to a former condition

_____ 8. To scatter in different directions

_____ 9. Relating to public speaking

_____ 10. Remorse or contrition

_____ 11. Uncertainly; hesitantly

_____ 12. Brought under control; quieted

_____ 13. To appease; make concessions

_____ 14. Relating to war

_____ 15. Showed indecision

_____ 16. Betrayal of one's country

_____ 17. Misbeliever; one who holds controversial opinions

_____ 18. Hanging back or falling behind

_____ 19. Those who work in return for instruction

_____ 20. Hated

Johnny Tremain Vocabulary Fill In The Blank 2 Answer Key

INSTIGATED	1. Started; initiated
PROTUBERANT	2. Swelling outward; bulging
DILAPIDATED	3. Broken-down
PIQUED	4. Felt wounded pride
CANNY	5. Careful and shrewd
ARDENT	6. Passionate; displaying a strong enthusiasm
REVERTED	7. Returned to a former condition
DISPERSE	8. To scatter in different directions
ORATORY	9. Relating to public speaking
REPENTANCE	10. Remorse or contrition
TENTATIVELY	11. Uncertainly; hesitantly
SUBDUED	12. Brought under control; quieted
PLACATE	13. To appease; make concessions
MARTIAL	14. Relating to war
WAVERED	15. Showed indecision
TREASON	16. Betrayal of one's country
HERETIC	17. Misbeliever; one who holds controversial opinions
LAGGARD	18. Hanging back or falling behind
APPRENTICES	19. Those who work in return for instruction
DETESTED	20. Hated

Johnny Tremain Vocabulary Fill In The Blank 3

1. Porcelain dish used for melting silver
2. Unpaid service to another
3. Uneasy feelings
4. Trading goods or services without money
5. Reduced in amount
6. Airy; fragile
7. Ordinary; boring
8. Standing idly about; lingering aimlessly
9. Started; initiated
10. Those who work in return for instruction
11. To appease; make concessions
12. Of little significance or value
13. Careful and shrewd
14. One whose welfare is promoted by another
15. Slowly; in a boring manner
16. Unconquerable
17. A public place for walking
18. Swelling outward; bulging
19. Expressing great pleasure or self-satisfaction
20. Relating to public speaking

Johnny Tremain Vocabulary Fill In The Blank 3 Answer Key

CRUCIBLE	1. Porcelain dish used for melting silver
INDENTURE	2. Unpaid service to another
QUALMS	3. Uneasy feelings
BARTERING	4. Trading goods or services without money
ABATED	5. Reduced in amount
ETHEREAL	6. Airy; fragile
MUNDANE	7. Ordinary; boring
LOITERING	8. Standing idly about; lingering aimlessly
INSTIGATED	9. Started; initiated
APPRENTICES	10. Those who work in return for instruction
PLACATE	11. To appease; make concessions
TRIVIAL	12. Of little significance or value
CANNY	13. Careful and shrewd
PROTEGEE	14. One whose welfare is promoted by another
TEDIOUSLY	15. Slowly; in a boring manner
INVINCIBLE	16. Unconquerable
PROMENADE	17. A public place for walking
PROTUBERANT	18. Swelling outward; bulging
GLOATING	19. Expressing great pleasure or self-satisfaction
ORATORY	20. Relating to public speaking

Johnny Tremain Vocabulary Fill In The Blank 4

_____ 1. Regrettable

_____ 2. Bell tower

_____ 3. Having loss of muscular control & sensation

_____ 4. Ordinary; boring

_____ 5. Unconquerable

_____ 6. Showed indecision

_____ 7. Hated

_____ 8. Careful and shrewd

_____ 9. Reasons for protest; complaints

_____ 10. Betrayal of one's country

_____ 11. A false action intended to deceive

_____ 12. Danger

_____ 13. An open revolt

_____ 14. Rebellious

_____ 15. Eager to fight; hostile

_____ 16. To scatter in different directions

_____ 17. Those who work in return for instruction

_____ 18. Returned to a former condition

_____ 19. Porcelain dish used for melting silver

_____ 20. A public place for walking

Johnny Tremain Vocabulary Fill In The Blank 4 Answer Key

LAMENTABLE	1. Regrettable
BELFRY	2. Bell tower
APOPLECTIC	3. Having loss of muscular control & sensation
MUNDANE	4. Ordinary; boring
INVINCIBLE	5. Unconquerable
WAVERED	6. Showed indecision
DETESTED	7. Hated
CANNY	8. Careful and shrewd
GRIEVANCES	9. Reasons for protest; complaints
TREASON	10. Betrayal of one's country
PRETENSE	11. A false action intended to deceive
PERIL	12. Danger
INSURRECTION	13. An open revolt
SEDITIOUS	14. Rebellious
BELLIGERENT	15. Eager to fight; hostile
DISPERSE	16. To scatter in different directions
APPRENTICES	17. Those who work in return for instruction
REVERTED	18. Returned to a former condition
CRUCIBLE	19. Porcelain dish used for melting silver
PROMENADE	20. A public place for walking

Johnny Tremain Vocabulary Matching 1

___ 1. LAMENTABLE   A. Standing idly about; lingering aimlessly
___ 2. CULTIVATE   B. Rebuked; scolded; put down
___ 3. TYRANNY   C. Relating to war
___ 4. MUNDANE   D. Alone
___ 5. LOITERING   E. Uncertainly; hesitantly
___ 6. CANNY   F. Regrettable
___ 7. DIFFIDENTLY   G. Inadequate strength or ability
___ 8. BARTERING   H. Careful and shrewd
___ 9. FLACCID   I. Boastfully
___10. SOLITARY   J. Trading goods or services without money
___11. AROUSE   K. Rebellious
___12. BERATED   L. Unjust use of absolute power
___13. ARROGANTLY   M. Brought under control; quieted
___14. INCAPACITY   N. Awaken or excite
___15. ORATORY   O. Relating to public speaking
___16. DETESTED   P. Hated
___17. MARTIAL   Q. Ghost
___18. APPARITION   R. Shyly; timidly
___19. LAGGARD   S. Airy; fragile
___20. TREASON   T. Hanging back or falling behind
___21. INSURRECTION   U. To nurture
___22. SUBDUED   V. An open revolt
___23. TENTATIVELY   W. Ordinary; boring
___24. SEDITIOUS   X. Lacking vigor or energy
___25. ETHEREAL   Y. Betrayal of one's country

Johnny Tremain Vocabulary Matching 1 Answer Key

F - 1. LAMENTABLE	A.	Standing idly about; lingering aimlessly
U - 2. CULTIVATE	B.	Rebuked; scolded; put down
L - 3. TYRANNY	C.	Relating to war
W - 4. MUNDANE	D.	Alone
A - 5. LOITERING	E.	Uncertainly; hesitantly
H - 6. CANNY	F.	Regrettable
R - 7. DIFFIDENTLY	G.	Inadequate strength or ability
J - 8. BARTERING	H.	Careful and shrewd
X - 9. FLACCID	I.	Boastfully
D - 10. SOLITARY	J.	Trading goods or services without money
N - 11. AROUSE	K.	Rebellious
B - 12. BERATED	L.	Unjust use of absolute power
I - 13. ARROGANTLY	M.	Brought under control; quieted
G - 14. INCAPACITY	N.	Awaken or excite
O - 15. ORATORY	O.	Relating to public speaking
P - 16. DETESTED	P.	Hated
C - 17. MARTIAL	Q.	Ghost
Q - 18. APPARITION	R.	Shyly; timidly
T - 19. LAGGARD	S.	Airy; fragile
Y - 20. TREASON	T.	Hanging back or falling behind
V - 21. INSURRECTION	U.	To nurture
M - 22. SUBDUED	V.	An open revolt
E - 23. TENTATIVELY	W.	Ordinary; boring
K - 24. SEDITIOUS	X.	Lacking vigor or energy
S - 25. ETHEREAL	Y.	Betrayal of one's country

Johnny Tremain Vocabulary Matching 2

___ 1. PLACATE
___ 2. STRIFE
___ 3. CULTIVATE
___ 4. IMPERCEPTIBLY
___ 5. BELFRY
___ 6. GRIEVANCES
___ 7. APOPLECTIC
___ 8. DETESTED
___ 9. TRIVIAL
___ 10. BARTERING
___ 11. INDOLENT
___ 12. ARSENAL
___ 13. INDENTURE
___ 14. PIQUED
___ 15. CIVIL
___ 16. DEMEANOR
___ 17. REPROVED
___ 18. LOITERING
___ 19. PARASITIC
___ 20. REPENTANCE
___ 21. PERIL
___ 22. PRETENSE
___ 23. MUNDANE
___ 24. CLAMOR
___ 25. DIFFIDENTLY

A. A struggle or fight
B. Relating to a citizen
C. Unpaid service to another
D. Felt wounded pride
E. Reasons for protest; complaints
F. Habitually lazy
G. A false action intended to deceive
H. Having loss of muscular control & sensation
I. To nurture
J. Ordinary; boring
K. A supply of weapons
L. Standing idly about; lingering aimlessly
M. Uproar
N. Remorse or contrition
O. Taking advantage of others without useful return
P. Shyly; timidly
Q. Bell tower
R. Trading goods or services without money
S. Found fault with
T. Danger
U. Of little significance or value
V. Hated
W. The way in which a person behaves
X. To appease; make concessions
Y. Not noticeably

Johnny Tremain Vocabulary Matching 2 Answer Key

X - 1. PLACATE	A. A struggle or fight
A - 2. STRIFE	B. Relating to a citizen
I - 3. CULTIVATE	C. Unpaid service to another
Y - 4. IMPERCEPTIBLY	D. Felt wounded pride
Q - 5. BELFRY	E. Reasons for protest; complaints
E - 6. GRIEVANCES	F. Habitually lazy
H - 7. APOPLECTIC	G. A false action intended to deceive
V - 8. DETESTED	H. Having loss of muscular control & sensation
U - 9. TRIVIAL	I. To nurture
R -10. BARTERING	J. Ordinary; boring
F -11. INDOLENT	K. A supply of weapons
K -12. ARSENAL	L. Standing idly about; lingering aimlessly
C -13. INDENTURE	M. Uproar
D -14. PIQUED	N. Remorse or contrition
B -15. CIVIL	O. Taking advantage of others without useful return
W -16. DEMEANOR	P. Shyly; timidly
S -17. REPROVED	Q. Bell tower
L -18. LOITERING	R. Trading goods or services without money
O -19. PARASITIC	S. Found fault with
N -20. REPENTANCE	T. Danger
T -21. PERIL	U. Of little significance or value
G -22. PRETENSE	V. Hated
J -23. MUNDANE	W. The way in which a person behaves
M -24. CLAMOR	X. To appease; make concessions
P -25. DIFFIDENTLY	Y. Not noticeably

Johnny Tremain Vocabulary Matching 3

___ 1. CRUCIBLE   A. Slowly; in a boring manner
___ 2. DEMEANOR   B. Expressing great pleasure or self-satisfaction
___ 3. TYRANNY   C. Having loss of muscular control & sensation
___ 4. INDOLENT   D. Unjust use of absolute power
___ 5. AVERTED   E. Unconsciously foolish
___ 6. DETESTED   F. Shyly; timidly
___ 7. INVINCIBLE   G. Alone
___ 8. CLAMOR   H. Ghost
___ 9. SOLITARY   I. Trading goods or services without money
___ 10. WARY   J. The way in which a person behaves
___ 11. ORATORY   K. Relating to public speaking
___ 12. DILIGENTLY   L. Regrettable
___ 13. TEDIOUSLY   M. Hated
___ 14. CORDIALLY   N. Porcelain dish used for melting silver
___ 15. BARTERING   O. Turned away
___ 16. ARSENAL   P. Uproar
___ 17. GLOATING   Q. Habitually lazy
___ 18. TENTATIVELY   R. In a hard-working manner
___ 19. APPARITION   S. Uncertainly; hesitantly
___ 20. LAMENTABLE   T. A supply of weapons
___ 21. TREASON   U. Betrayal of one's country
___ 22. DIFFIDENTLY   V. Cheerlessly; gloomily
___ 23. APOPLECTIC   W. Sincerely; warmly
___ 24. FATUOUS   X. On guard; watchful
___ 25. DISCONSOLATELY   Y. Unconquerable

Johnny Tremain Vocabulary Matching 3 Answer Key

N - 1. CRUCIBLE		A. Slowly; in a boring manner
J - 2. DEMEANOR		B. Expressing great pleasure or self-satisfaction
D - 3. TYRANNY		C. Having loss of muscular control & sensation
Q - 4. INDOLENT		D. Unjust use of absolute power
O - 5. AVERTED		E. Unconsciously foolish
M - 6. DETESTED		F. Shyly; timidly
Y - 7. INVINCIBLE		G. Alone
P - 8. CLAMOR		H. Ghost
G - 9. SOLITARY		I. Trading goods or services without money
X - 10. WARY		J. The way in which a person behaves
K - 11. ORATORY		K. Relating to public speaking
R - 12. DILIGENTLY		L. Regrettable
A - 13. TEDIOUSLY		M. Hated
W - 14. CORDIALLY		N. Porcelain dish used for melting silver
I - 15. BARTERING		O. Turned away
T - 16. ARSENAL		P. Uproar
B - 17. GLOATING		Q. Habitually lazy
S - 18. TENTATIVELY		R. In a hard-working manner
H - 19. APPARITION		S. Uncertainly; hesitantly
L - 20. LAMENTABLE		T. A supply of weapons
U - 21. TREASON		U. Betrayal of one's country
F - 22. DIFFIDENTLY		V. Cheerlessly; gloomily
C - 23. APOPLECTIC		W. Sincerely; warmly
E - 24. FATUOUS		X. On guard; watchful
V - 25. DISCONSOLATELY		Y. Unconquerable

Johnny Tremain Vocabulary Matching 4

___ 1. GLOATING   A. Taking advantage of others without useful return
___ 2. SEDITIOUS   B. Ordinary; boring
___ 3. PROMENADE   C. A public place for walking
___ 4. INCAPACITY   D. Showed indecision
___ 5. REPROVED   E. Expressing great pleasure or self-satisfaction
___ 6. SURFEITED   F. Inadequate strength or ability
___ 7. PROTUBERANT   G. Found fault with
___ 8. MUNDANE   H. Slowly; in a boring manner
___ 9. INVINCIBLE   I. Swelling outward; bulging
___10. PIETY   J. Rebellious
___11. CRUCIBLE   K. Turned away
___12. ENIGMATICAL   L. Airy; fragile
___13. APOPLECTIC   M. Having loss of muscular control & sensation
___14. FLACCID   N. Porcelain dish used for melting silver
___15. AVERTED   O. Unconquerable
___16. PARASITIC   P. Reverence
___17. APPRENTICES   Q. Saturated; overfilled
___18. LAMENTABLE   R. Relating to public speaking
___19. CLAMOR   S. Lacking vigor or energy
___20. ORATORY   T. Shyly; timidly
___21. WAVERED   U. Those who work in return for instruction
___22. ETHEREAL   V. Puzzling
___23. WARY   W. Regrettable
___24. TEDIOUSLY   X. Uproar
___25. DIFFIDENTLY   Y. On guard; watchful

Johnny Tremain Vocabulary Matching 4 Answer Key

E - 1. GLOATING	A. Taking advantage of others without useful return
J - 2. SEDITIOUS	B. Ordinary; boring
C - 3. PROMENADE	C. A public place for walking
F - 4. INCAPACITY	D. Showed indecision
G - 5. REPROVED	E. Expressing great pleasure or self-satisfaction
Q - 6. SURFEITED	F. Inadequate strength or ability
I - 7. PROTUBERANT	G. Found fault with
B - 8. MUNDANE	H. Slowly; in a boring manner
O - 9. INVINCIBLE	I. Swelling outward; bulging
P - 10. PIETY	J. Rebellious
N - 11. CRUCIBLE	K. Turned away
V - 12. ENIGMATICAL	L. Airy; fragile
M - 13. APOPLECTIC	M. Having loss of muscular control & sensation
S - 14. FLACCID	N. Porcelain dish used for melting silver
K - 15. AVERTED	O. Unconquerable
A - 16. PARASITIC	P. Reverence
U - 17. APPRENTICES	Q. Saturated; overfilled
W - 18. LAMENTABLE	R. Relating to public speaking
X - 19. CLAMOR	S. Lacking vigor or energy
R - 20. ORATORY	T. Shyly; timidly
D - 21. WAVERED	U. Those who work in return for instruction
L - 22. ETHEREAL	V. Puzzling
Y - 23. WARY	W. Regrettable
H - 24. TEDIOUSLY	X. Uproar
T - 25. DIFFIDENTLY	Y. On guard; watchful

Johnny Tremain Vocabulary Magic Squares 1

Match the definition with the vocabulary word. Put your answers in the magic squares below. When your answers are correct, all columns and rows will add to the same number.

A. PIETY
B. AROUSE
C. FATUOUS
D. PARASITIC
E. POULTICE
F. INDENTURE
G. BELLIGERENT
H. DISPERSE
I. INUNDATED
J. INSTIGATED
K. PROTEGEE
L. FLACCID
M. PROTUBERANT
N. CONCOCTION
O. TREASON
P. INSURRECTION

1. Unpaid service to another
2. Overwhelmed; swamped
3. Betrayal of one's country
4. Taking advantage of others without useful return
5. Swelling outward; bulging
6. Awaken or excite
7. To scatter in different directions
8. One whose welfare is promoted by another
9. Unconsciously foolish
10. An open revolt
11. Started; initiated
12. Dressing for a wound or injury
13. Lacking vigor or energy
14. Eager to fight; hostile
15. Reverence
16. Food or beverage made of mixed ingredients

A=	B=	C=	D=
E=	F=	G=	H=
I=	J=	K=	L=
M=	N=	O=	P=

Johnny Tremain Vocabulary Magic Squares 1 Answer Key

Match the definition with the vocabulary word. Put your answers in the magic squares below. When your answers are correct, all columns and rows will add to the same number.

A. PIETY
B. AROUSE
C. FATUOUS
D. PARASITIC
E. POULTICE
F. INDENTURE
G. BELLIGERENT
H. DISPERSE
I. INUNDATED
J. INSTIGATED
K. PROTEGEE
L. FLACCID
M. PROTUBERANT
N. CONCOCTION
O. TREASON
P. INSURRECTION

1. Unpaid service to another
2. Overwhelmed; swamped
3. Betrayal of one's country
4. Taking advantage of others without useful return
5. Swelling outward; bulging
6. Awaken or excite
7. To scatter in different directions
8. One whose welfare is promoted by another
9. Unconsciously foolish
10. An open revolt
11. Started; initiated
12. Dressing for a wound or injury
13. Lacking vigor or energy
14. Eager to fight; hostile
15. Reverence
16. Food or beverage made of mixed ingredients

A=15	B=6	C=9	D=4
E=12	F=1	G=14	H=7
I=2	J=11	K=8	L=13
M=5	N=16	O=3	P=10

Johnny Tremain Vocabulary Magic Squares 2

Match the definition with the vocabulary word. Put your answers in the magic squares below. When your answers are correct, all columns and rows will add to the same number.

A. BELLIGERENT
B. CIVIL
C. GLOATING
D. ARDENT
E. CONCOCTION
F. HERETIC
G. SUBDUED
H. SEDITIOUS
I. DISCONSOLATELY
J. REPROVED
K. QUALMS
L. INCAPACITY
M. SURFEITED
N. DEMEANOR
O. TREASON
P. PRETENSE

1. Relating to a citizen
2. Brought under control; quieted
3. Uneasy feelings
4. The way in which a person behaves
5. Saturated; overfilled
6. Inadequate strength or ability
7. Rebellious
8. Eager to fight; hostile
9. A false action intended to deceive
10. Cheerlessly; gloomily
11. Food or beverage made of mixed ingredients
12. Passionate; displaying a strong enthusiasm
13. Expressing great pleasure or self-satisfaction
14. Misbeliever; one who holds controversial opinions
15. Found fault with
16. Betrayal of one's country

A=	B=	C=	D=
E=	F=	G=	H=
I=	J=	K=	L=
M=	N=	O=	P=

Johnny Tremain Vocabulary Magic Squares 2 Answer Key

Match the definition with the vocabulary word. Put your answers in the magic squares below. When your answers are correct, all columns and rows will add to the same number.

A. BELLIGERENT
B. CIVIL
C. GLOATING
D. ARDENT
E. CONCOCTION
F. HERETIC
G. SUBDUED
H. SEDITIOUS
I. DISCONSOLATELY
J. REPROVED
K. QUALMS
L. INCAPACITY
M. SURFEITED
N. DEMEANOR
O. TREASON
P. PRETENSE

1. Relating to a citizen
2. Brought under control; quieted
3. Uneasy feelings
4. The way in which a person behaves
5. Saturated; overfilled
6. Inadequate strength or ability
7. Rebellious
8. Eager to fight; hostile
9. A false action intended to deceive
10. Cheerlessly; gloomily
11. Food or beverage made of mixed ingredients
12. Passionate; displaying a strong enthusiasm
13. Expressing great pleasure or self-satisfaction
14. Misbeliever; one who holds controversial opinions
15. Found fault with
16. Betrayal of one's country

A=8	B=1	C=13	D=12
E=11	F=14	G=2	H=7
I=10	J=15	K=3	L=6
M=5	N=4	O=16	P=9

Johnny Tremain Vocabulary Magic Squares 3

Match the definition with the vocabulary word. Put your answers in the magic squares below. When your answers are correct, all columns and rows will add to the same number.

A. SEDITIOUS
B. APPARITION
C. PARASITIC
D. TENTATIVELY
E. REPENTANCE
F. CULTIVATE
G. PUNCTILIOUS
H. PRODIGIOUSLY
I. LAGGARD
J. CANNY
K. BARTERING
L. AROUSE
M. LUCID
N. BELLIGERENT
O. TREASON
P. PROMENADE

1. Eager to fight; hostile
2. Precise; scrupulous
3. Awaken or excite
4. Rebellious
5. Trading goods or services without money
6. Ghost
7. Easily understood; intelligible
8. In an impressively great way
9. Remorse or contrition
10. A public place for walking
11. Taking advantage of others without useful return
12. Careful and shrewd
13. Uncertainly; hesitantly
14. Hanging back or falling behind
15. To nurture
16. Betrayal of one's country

A=	B=	C=	D=
E=	F=	G=	H=
I=	J=	K=	L=
M=	N=	O=	P=

Johnny Tremain Vocabulary Magic Squares 3 Answer Key

Match the definition with the vocabulary word. Put your answers in the magic squares below. When your answers are correct, all columns and rows will add to the same number.

A. SEDITIOUS
B. APPARITION
C. PARASITIC
D. TENTATIVELY
E. REPENTANCE
F. CULTIVATE
G. PUNCTILIOUS
H. PRODIGIOUSLY
I. LAGGARD
J. CANNY
K. BARTERING
L. AROUSE
M. LUCID
N. BELLIGERENT
O. TREASON
P. PROMENADE

1. Eager to fight; hostile
2. Precise; scrupulous
3. Awaken or excite
4. Rebellious
5. Trading goods or services without money
6. Ghost
7. Easily understood; intelligible
8. In an impressively great way
9. Remorse or contrition
10. A public place for walking
11. Taking advantage of others without useful return
12. Careful and shrewd
13. Uncertainly; hesitantly
14. Hanging back or falling behind
15. To nurture
16. Betrayal of one's country

A=4	B=6	C=11	D=13
E=9	F=15	G=2	H=8
I=14	J=12	K=5	L=3
M=7	N=1	O=16	P=10

Johnny Tremain Vocabulary Magic Squares 4

Match the definition with the vocabulary word. Put your answers in the magic squares below. When your answers are correct, all columns and rows will add to the same number.

A. REPENTANCE
B. PIQUED
C. PIETY
D. DEMEANOR
E. MARTIAL
F. DISPERSE
G. STRIFE
H. COMPASSIONATE
I. PROTUBERANT
J. PAROXYSM
K. AROUSE
L. ENIGMATICAL
M. BARTERING
N. DILIGENTLY
O. TREASON
P. INUNDATED

1. Sympathetic
2. Trading goods or services without money
3. Felt wounded pride
4. Awaken or excite
5. A spasm or fit
6. Reverence
7. Overwhelmed; swamped
8. Relating to war
9. Betrayal of one's country
10. To scatter in different directions
11. Swelling outward; bulging
12. The way in which a person behaves
13. Remorse or contrition
14. Puzzling
15. A struggle or fight
16. In a hard-working manner

A=	B=	C=	D=
E=	F=	G=	H=
I=	J=	K=	L=
M=	N=	O=	P=

Johnny Tremain Vocabulary Magic Squares 4 Answer Key

Match the definition with the vocabulary word. Put your answers in the magic squares below. When your answers are correct, all columns and rows will add to the same number.

A. REPENTANCE
B. PIQUED
C. PIETY
D. DEMEANOR
E. MARTIAL
F. DISPERSE
G. STRIFE
H. COMPASSIONATE
I. PROTUBERANT
J. PAROXYSM
K. AROUSE
L. ENIGMATICAL
M. BARTERING
N. DILIGENTLY
O. TREASON
P. INUNDATED

1. Sympathetic
2. Trading goods or services without money
3. Felt wounded pride
4. Awaken or excite
5. A spasm or fit
6. Reverence
7. Overwhelmed; swamped
8. Relating to war
9. Betrayal of one's country
10. To scatter in different directions
11. Swelling outward; bulging
12. The way in which a person behaves
13. Remorse or contrition
14. Puzzling
15. A struggle or fight
16. In a hard-working manner

A=13	B=3	C=6	D=12
E=8	F=10	G=15	H=1
I=11	J=5	K=4	L=14
M=2	N=16	O=9	P=7

Johnny Tremain Vocabulary Word Search 1

```
S U B D U E D T R E A S O N L I R E P R
L G Q H F T M X F L A C C I D K O S L T
B R P E S O L I T A R Y V T W E N R A C
Y I D R A G G A L T C I T C Q C A E C B
L E E E O D B T B U C P B M Z N E P A Y
E V T T M T B C A R S N R L G A M S T H
V A A I T U E D W B M X R O E T E I E V
I N G C A P N G I U A B H P M N D D Z V
T C I V M R O D E L D T E P P E I S R X
A E T S Z M D U A E I R E L I P N E Y S
T S S D B B H E L N U G T D F E P A N Y
N O N C H A L A N T E R E V E R T E D T
E T I X N B F W N T I T W N O D Y Y C E
T H P B I N L E H V S C Y V T J W N A K
S K B C Z A D E I E G S E P A L K Y N Z
C T U Z I N R A T F M D D J B R Y X N K
H R R T I E L E H L P I Q U E D O Q Y S
C Y R I A L D Y A W C D E T A D N U N I
L A Y L F A T U O U S E D I T I O U S P
M W A R Y E Q C L A M O R A T O R Y J E
```

A public place for walking (9)
A struggle or fight (6)
Airy; fragile (8)
Alone (8)
Awaken or excite (6)
Bell tower (6)
Betrayal of one's country (7)
Brought under control; quieted (7)
Careful and shrewd (5)
Danger (5)
To scatter in different directions (8)
Dressing for a wound or injury (8)
Easily understood; intelligible (5)
Felt wounded pride (6)
Found fault with (8)
Hanging back or falling behind (7)
Hated (8)
In a hard-working manner (10)
Lacking vigor or energy (7)
Merciful; indulgent (7)
Misbeliever; one who holds controversial opinions (7)
Of little significance or value (7)
On guard; watchful (4)
One whose welfare is promoted by another (8)

Ordinary; boring (7)
Overwhelmed; swamped (9)
Passionate; displaying a strong enthusiasm (6)
Porcelain dish used for melting silver (8)
Reasons for protest; complaints (10)
Rebellious (9)
Reduced in amount (6)
Relating to a citizen (5)
Relating to public speaking (7)
Relating to war (7)
Remorse or contrition (10)
Returned to a former condition (8)
Reverence (5)
Started; initiated (10)
The way in which a person behaves (8)
To appease; make concessions (7)
Uncertainly; hesitantly (11)
Unconcerned or indifferent (10)
Unconsciously foolish (7)
Uneasy feelings (6)
Unpaid service to another (9)
Uproar (6)
Violently agitated or disturbed (9)

Johnny Tremain Vocabulary Word Search 1 Answer Key

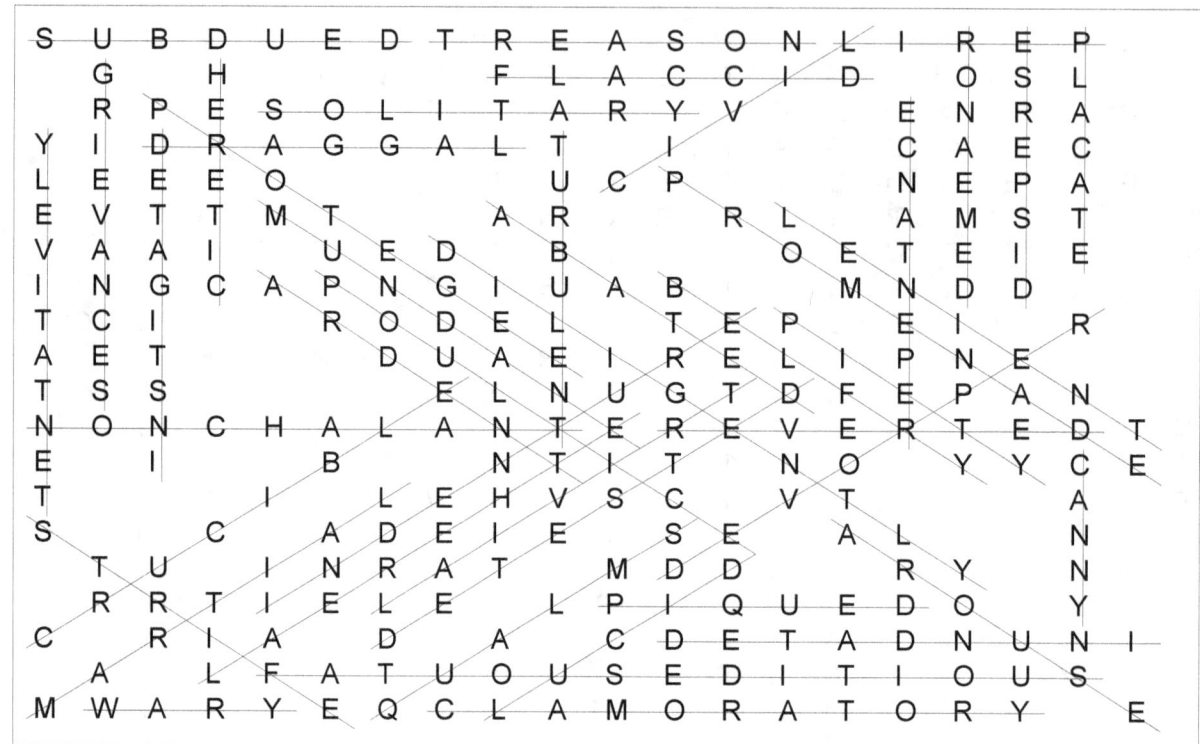

A public place for walking (9)
A struggle or fight (6)
Airy; fragile (8)
Alone (8)
Awaken or excite (6)
Bell tower (6)
Betrayal of one's country (7)
Brought under control; quieted (7)
Careful and shrewd (5)
Danger (5)
To scatter in different directions (8)
Dressing for a wound or injury (8)
Easily understood; intelligible (5)
Felt wounded pride (6)
Found fault with (8)
Hanging back or falling behind (7)
Hated (8)
In a hard-working manner (10)
Lacking vigor or energy (7)
Merciful; indulgent (7)
Misbeliever; one who holds controversial opinions (7)
Of little significance or value (7)
On guard; watchful (4)
One whose welfare is promoted by another (8)

Ordinary; boring (7)
Overwhelmed; swamped (9)
Passionate; displaying a strong enthusiasm (6)
Porcelain dish used for melting silver (8)
Reasons for protest; complaints (10)
Rebellious (9)
Reduced in amount (6)
Relating to a citizen (5)
Relating to public speaking (7)
Relating to war (7)
Remorse or contrition (10)
Returned to a former condition (8)
Reverence (5)
Started; initiated (10)
The way in which a person behaves (8)
To appease; make concessions (7)
Uncertainly; hesitantly (11)
Unconcerned or indifferent (10)
Unconsciously foolish (7)
Uneasy feelings (6)
Unpaid service to another (9)
Uproar (6)
Violently agitated or disturbed (9)

Johnny Tremain Vocabulary Word Search 2

```
I M P E R C E P T I B L Y A V E R T E D
N Y F E P I C Y D E E A T J R C A N N Y
U D W G P V N J R R L E R O R O M A L C
N J X E J I A A A E F R I G R P U D S N
D W M T K L T J G P R E V R Z A T S D W
A V L O T E N D G R Y H I I G T I E J
T P W R D Q E L A O P T A E N K S O G P
E I P P X B P F L V N E L V D C H C R A
D N P A F L E L D E T A B A O V T E R Y
J D R B R T R A N D S B G N L K T D R M
H E R E T I C C S E Z T S C E E E I J W
Y N N A R Y T C C O P O P E N N T F R X
P T E N T A T I V E L Y I S T R I F E B
B U P Y C L T D O A A I E Y Z V A I N G
C R B G F N F N T N C W T Q L T Q D A H
L E N I E N T E L W A R Y A U X U E D P
S T Y R V Q L I U M T L B O R W A N V
X L P L K Y R R C M E D U S C Y L T U N
S P Y N B E F Z I A R S E N A L M L M L
A S M S P N S M D E U Q I P F L S Y V T
```

A false action intended to deceive (8)
A struggle or fight (6)
A supply of weapons (7)
Airy; fragile (8)
Alone (8)
Awaken or excite (6)
Bell tower (6)
Careful and shrewd (5)
Cheerlessly; gloomily (14)
Danger (5)
Easily understood; intelligible (5)
Felt wounded pride (6)
Found fault with (8)
Ghost (10)
Habitually lazy (8)
Hanging back or falling behind (7)
Lacking vigor or energy (7)
Merciful; indulgent (7)
Misbeliever; one who holds controversial opinions (7)
Not noticeably (13)
Of little significance or value (7)
On guard; watchful (4)
One whose welfare is promoted by another (8)
Ordinary; boring (7)

Overwhelmed; swamped (9)
Passionate; displaying a strong enthusiasm (6)
Reasons for protest; complaints (10)
Rebuked; scolded; put down (7)
Reduced in amount (6)
Relating to a citizen (5)
Relating to public speaking (7)
Remorse or contrition (10)
Reverence (5)
Shyly; timidly (11)
Those who work in return for instruction (11)
To appease; make concessions (7)
Turned away (7)
Uncertainly; hesitantly (11)
Unconsciously foolish (7)
Uneasy feelings (6)
Unjust use of absolute power (7)
Unpaid service to another (9)
Uproar (6)

Johnny Tremain Vocabulary Word Search 2 Answer Key

A false action intended to deceive (8)
A struggle or fight (6)
A supply of weapons (7)
Airy; fragile (8)
Alone (8)
Awaken or excite (6)
Bell tower (6)
Careful and shrewd (5)
Cheerlessly; gloomily (14)
Danger (5)
Easily understood; intelligible (5)
Felt wounded pride (6)
Found fault with (8)
Ghost (10)
Habitually lazy (8)
Hanging back or falling behind (7)
Lacking vigor or energy (7)
Merciful; indulgent (7)
Misbeliever; one who holds controversial opinions (7)
Not noticeably (13)
Of little significance or value (7)
On guard; watchful (4)
One whose welfare is promoted by another (8)
Ordinary; boring (7)

Overwhelmed; swamped (9)
Passionate; displaying a strong enthusiasm (6)
Reasons for protest; complaints (10)
Rebuked; scolded; put down (7)
Reduced in amount (6)
Relating to a citizen (5)
Relating to public speaking (7)
Remorse or contrition (10)
Reverence (5)
Shyly; timidly (11)
Those who work in return for instruction (11)
To appease; make concessions (7)
Turned away (7)
Uncertainly; hesitantly (11)
Unconsciously foolish (7)
Uneasy feelings (6)
Unjust use of absolute power (7)
Unpaid service to another (9)
Uproar (6)

Johnny Tremain Vocabulary Word Search 3

```
I N D E N T U R E Y L R E P R O V E D H
S F L A C C I D G C A A R T H S T Q C G
H L V R B N K N H X I O R S R S T X L D
C Y K D I L I G E N T L Y O T J M C A Q
T U W E F R L N F E R T G Y U R P Z M V
S Z L N E M B A G L A K E N X S I D O P
U D E T E S T E D X M U N D A N E F R N
O N I P I U E D C S N T W E I T T T E C
I O Y C O V E D Y L L A A T A O Y M P T
L S S U G T A X J A Q G V R Q G U C G C
I A S E A J O T C N M M E E Y N S S P M
T E T B D R J I E E T B R V R I L C L X
C R A U A I T H V S M E E F T Q O C Y
N T I P R A T L B R G Y D R L A E R A M
U K N V M B A I A A N R R K E O Z D N W
P S Z G I E U W O G B O I A B L F I N F
W X I Y R A W L E U G T F E N G Y A Y K
D N P E Z T L S E Q S A R P V N P L P M
E B H E X N R U T N E R R D N A Y L R C
M T H R E T I C T T O E D L D N Y E K
E F M L P I B Z A I T U Q I E C F C T T
A M P S L N L C P D D C V U B J T W E Z
N L I F M E A J L B M I Q U A L M S N S
O D Q B L L F B U E C I T L U O P P S R
R C J G P G C S L A P P R E N T I C E S
```

ABATED	CORDIALLY	GRIEVANCES	PERIL	SEDITIOUS
APPRENTICES	CULTIVATE	HERETIC	PIETY	STRIFE
ARDENT	DEMEANOR	INDENTURE	PIQUED	SUBDUED
AROUSE	DETESTED	LAGGARD	PLACATE	TEDIOUSLY
ARSENAL	DILIGENTLY	LENIENT	POULTICE	TREASON
AVERTED	DISPERSE	LOITERING	PRETENSE	TRIVIAL
BELFRY	ENIGMATICAL	LUCID	PROTEGEE	TURBULENT
BERATED	ETHEREAL	MARTIAL	PUNCTILIOUS	TYRANNY
CANNY	FATUOUS	MUNDANE	QUALMS	WARY
CIVIL	FLACCID	ORATORY	REPROVED	WAVERED
CLAMOR	GLOATING	PAROXYSM	REVERTED	

Johnny Tremain Vocabulary Word Search 3 Answer Key

```
I  N  D  E  N  T  U  R  E        L     R  E  P  R  O  V  E  D
   F  L  A  C  C  I  D        G  A     R                    C
      R              N           I  O  R  S                 L
C        D  I  L  I  G  E  N  T  L  Y  O  T                 A
   U     E     R        F  E  R  T     U  R     P           M
S     L  N  E        A  G  A  I     U  S  I     D           O
U  D  E  T  E  S  T  E  D  M  U  N  D  A  N  E  F           R
O  N  I     I  U  E  D     S     W  E  I  T  O  U           E
I  O     O  V  E     T  Y  L  L  A  T  A  G  Y
L  S  S  U  T  A  X     A  A     V  R  Y  N  U     S
I  E  E  A  B  D  R     I  E     E  E  F  I  T     C
T  R  B  U  A  I  T     L  S  T  B  E  L  A  O     O     Y
C  A  U  P  R  A  T  L  A  R  G  Y  D  R  E  L  E  R  D  C
N  T  I  V  M  B  A  I  I  O  R  R  I  B  A  R  A  D  I  A
U     P  G  I  E  U  O  G  T  R  O  A  E  L  G     I  I  N
P     I  Y  R  A  W  L  E  U  G  T  E  N  V  N     A  A  N
   D  N  P  E  T  L  S  N  R  T  D  R  D  Y  N     L  L  Y
D  E  H  E  R  E  T  I  C  T  O  E  D  L  N        L  L  P
E  M  T  H  E  R  E  T  I  C  T  O  E  D  L  N     Y  C  R
E           P     I  N  L  A     U     I        V  U  E
A           S     E  L  C  A     D  U     Q  U  A  L  M  S  N
N                                B        I     T  L  U  O  P  S
O  D                       U  E  C  I  T  L  U  O  P        E
R              P           S     A  P  P  R  E  N  T  I  C  E  S
```

ABATED	CORDIALLY	GRIEVANCES	PERIL	SEDITIOUS
APPRENTICES	CULTIVATE	HERETIC	PIETY	STRIFE
ARDENT	DEMEANOR	INDENTURE	PIQUED	SUBDUED
AROUSE	DETESTED	LAGGARD	PLACATE	TEDIOUSLY
ARSENAL	DILIGENTLY	LENIENT	POULTICE	TREASON
AVERTED	DISPERSE	LOITERING	PRETENSE	TRIVIAL
BELFRY	ENIGMATICAL	LUCID	PROTEGEE	TURBULENT
BERATED	ETHEREAL	MARTIAL	PUNCTILIOUS	TYRANNY
CANNY	FATUOUS	MUNDANE	QUALMS	WARY
CIVIL	FLACCID	ORATORY	REPROVED	WAVERED
CLAMOR	GLOATING	PAROXYSM	REVERTED	

Johnny Tremain Vocabulary Word Search 4

```
D L P A Y N N A R Y T P P A R O X Y S M
E G L B S O L I T A R Y R O M A L C U C
T I A A J R U I R I L L O E S D V C R Z
A N C T T Q C Q I E N S M L T L Z J F C
D D A E P A I D V J Q U E A V E R T E D
I O T D P Z D I I Y S O N N M F N T I H
P L E A Y K T D A F R I A D F I Y S T C
A E C S G A W K L Y F G D B A R Y G E T
L N C I T I S A R A P I E A O T Z X D N
I T D N N H J P R Y F D D T R S E I I M
D W E V E N H P W Y S O A E V O S D L W
P T F N D E R R B H G R P B N C U M I H
N C P Y R F L E B A O P E I O T N S G Z
L D O E A F A N V H R T I N E O L R E N
G N T M R V D T C E H T S Q I T I Y N C
B I P A P I Z I U E R O E T U E Y S T E
C N O R C A L C R O L T C R V E J U L L
U X U T A D S E W A U O E A I J D B Y V
L C L I N P A S T F C S N D D N A D Y R
T C T A N L M E I N P C R E S T G U H F
I J I L Y N L V O O E W T M N B S E Q C
V Z C V J Y K C P S N A L E P B P D W F
A S E D I T I O U S R A M F L A C C I D
T U R B U L E N T E U A T R E A S O N R
E E G E T O R P B Q L S B E N A D N U M
```

ABATED	DIFFIDENTLY	MARTIAL	QUALMS
APPRENTICES	DILAPIDATED	MUNDANE	REVERTED
ARDENT	DILIGENTLY	ORATORY	SEDITIOUS
AROUSE	DISCONSOLATELY	PARASITIC	SOLITARY
AVERTED	ETHEREAL	PAROXYSM	STRIFE
BARTERING	FATUOUS	PERIL	SUBDUED
BELFRY	FLACCID	PIETY	SURFEITED
BERATED	GRIEVANCES	PIQUED	TENTATIVELY
CANNY	HERETIC	PLACATE	TREASON
CIVIL	INCAPACITY	POULTICE	TRIVIAL
CLAMOR	INDOLENT	PRETENSE	TURBULENT
COMPASSIONATE	INUNDATED	PRODIGIOUSLY	TYRANNY
CONCOCTION	LAMENTABLE	PROMENADE	WARY
CULTIVATE	LUCID	PROTEGEE	

Johnny Tremain Vocabulary Word Search 4 Answer Key

ABATED	DIFFIDENTLY	MARTIAL	QUALMS
APPRENTICES	DILAPIDATED	MUNDANE	REVERTED
ARDENT	DILIGENTLY	ORATORY	SEDITIOUS
AROUSE	DISCONSOLATELY	PARASITIC	SOLITARY
AVERTED	ETHEREAL	PAROXYSM	STRIFE
BARTERING	FATUOUS	PERIL	SUBDUED
BELFRY	FLACCID	PIETY	SURFEITED
BERATED	GRIEVANCES	PIQUED	TENTATIVELY
CANNY	HERETIC	PLACATE	TREASON
CIVIL	INCAPACITY	POULTICE	TRIVIAL
CLAMOR	INDOLENT	PRETENSE	TURBULENT
COMPASSIONATE	INUNDATED	PRODIGIOUSLY	TYRANNY
CONCOCTION	LAMENTABLE	PROMENADE	WARY
CULTIVATE	LUCID	PROTEGEE	

Johnny Tremain Vocabulary Crossword 1

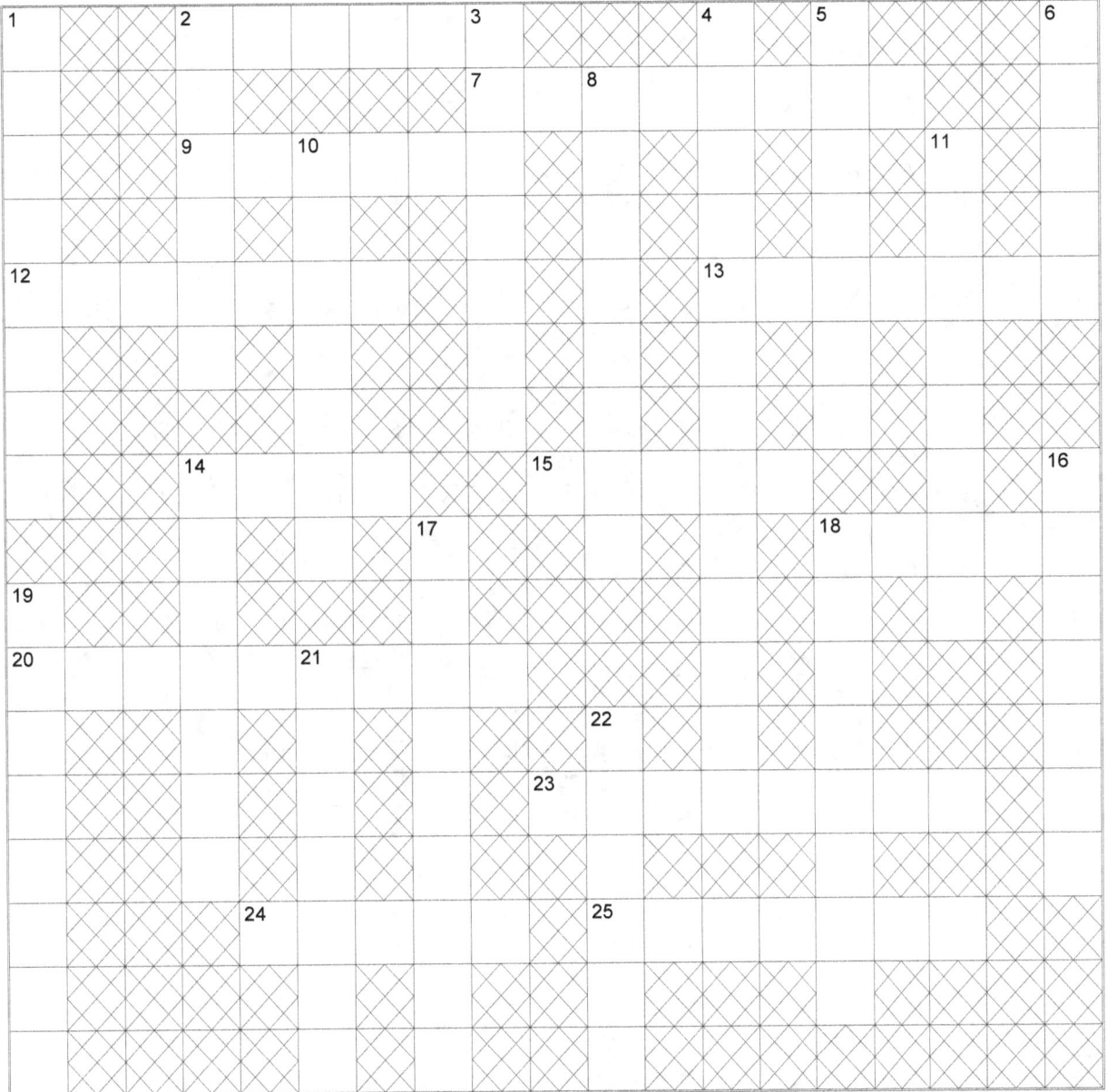

Across
2. Passionate; displaying a strong enthusiasm
7. Found fault with
9. Awaken or excite
12. A supply of weapons
13. Turned away
14. On guard; watchful
15. Danger
18. Reverence
20. Unpaid service to another
23. Returned to a former condition
24. Relating to a citizen
25. Lacking vigor or energy

Down
1. The way in which a person behaves
2. Reduced in amount
3. Betrayal of one's country
4. Sympathetic
5. Merciful; indulgent
6. Easily understood; intelligible
8. One whose welfare is promoted by another
10. Relating to public speaking
11. Hated
14. Showed indecision
16. Unjust use of absolute power
17. Trading goods or services without money
18. Dressing for a wound or injury
19. To scatter in different directions
21. Of little significance or value
22. Bell tower

Johnny Tremain Vocabulary Crossword 1 Answer Key

	1 D		2 A	R	D	E	N	3 T			4 C		5 L			6 L
	E		B				7 R	E	8 P	R	O	V	E	D		U
	M		9 A	R	10 O	U	S	E		R	M		N		11 D	C
	E		T		R			A		O	P		I		E	I
12 A	R	S	E	N	A	L		S		T	13 A	V	E	R	T	E	D
N			D		T			O		E	S		N		E	
O					O			N		G	S		T		S	
R			14 W	A	R	Y		15 P	E	R	I	L			16 T
			A		Y		17 B	E		O		18 P	I	E	T	Y
19 D			V				A			N		O	D		R
20 I	N	D	E	N	21 T	U	R	E			A		U		A
S			R		R		T		22 B		T		L		N
P			E		I		E		23 R	E	V	E	R	T	E	D	N
E			D		V		R		L		I				Y
R			24 C	I	V	I	L		25 F	L	A	C	C	I	D
S					A		N		R		E			
E					L		G		Y					

Across
2. Passionate; displaying a strong enthusiasm
7. Found fault with
9. Awaken or excite
12. A supply of weapons
13. Turned away
14. On guard; watchful
15. Danger
18. Reverence
20. Unpaid service to another
23. Returned to a former condition
24. Relating to a citizen
25. Lacking vigor or energy

Down
1. The way in which a person behaves
2. Reduced in amount
3. Betrayal of one's country
4. Sympathetic
5. Merciful; indulgent
6. Easily understood; intelligible
8. One whose welfare is promoted by another
10. Relating to public speaking
11. Hated
14. Showed indecision
16. Unjust use of absolute power
17. Trading goods or services without money
18. Dressing for a wound or injury
19. To scatter in different directions
21. Of little significance or value
22. Bell tower

Johnny Tremain Vocabulary Crossword 2

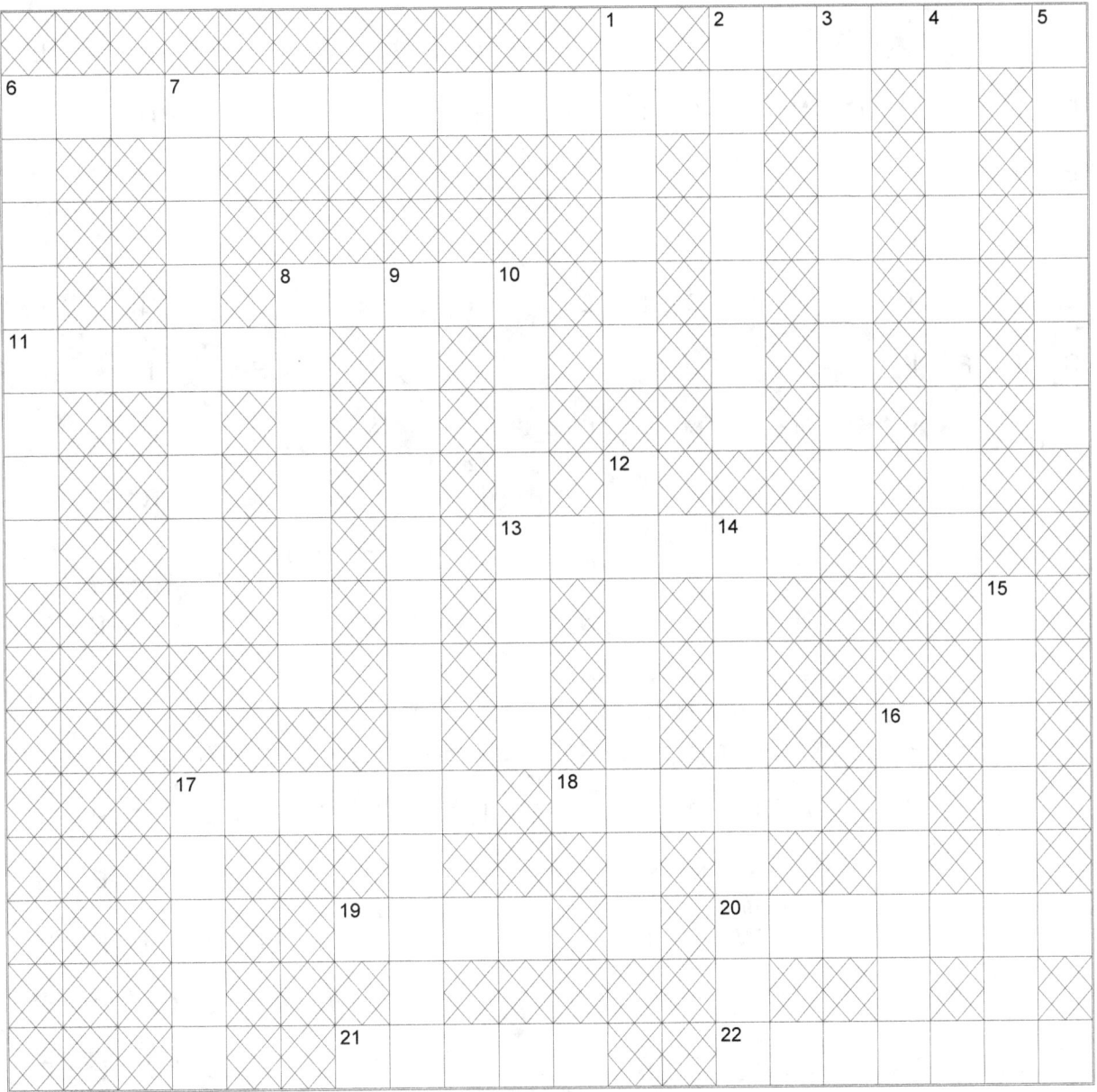

Across
2. Of little significance or value
6. Cheerlessly; gloomily
8. Easily understood; intelligible
11. A struggle or fight
13. Awaken or excite
17. Uproar
18. Reverence
19. On guard; watchful
20. Relating to public speaking
21. Danger
22. Brought under control; quieted

Down
1. Bell tower
2. Unjust use of absolute power
3. Habitually lazy
4. Unpaid service to another
5. Hanging back or falling behind
6. Hated
7. To nurture
8. Merciful; indulgent
9. Sympathetic
10. The way in which a person behaves
12. Dressing for a wound or injury
14. Rebellious
15. To scatter in different directions
16. Reduced in amount
17. Careful and shrewd

Johnny Tremain Vocabulary Crossword 2 Answer Key

Across
2. Of little significance or value
6. Cheerlessly; gloomily
8. Easily understood; intelligible
11. A struggle or fight
13. Awaken or excite
17. Uproar
18. Reverence
19. On guard; watchful
20. Relating to public speaking
21. Danger
22. Brought under control; quieted

Down
1. Bell tower
2. Unjust use of absolute power
3. Habitually lazy
4. Unpaid service to another
5. Hanging back or falling behind
6. Hated
7. To nurture
8. Merciful; indulgent
9. Sympathetic
10. The way in which a person behaves
12. Dressing for a wound or injury
14. Rebellious
15. To scatter in different directions
16. Reduced in amount
17. Careful and shrewd

Johnny Tremain Vocabulary Crossword 3

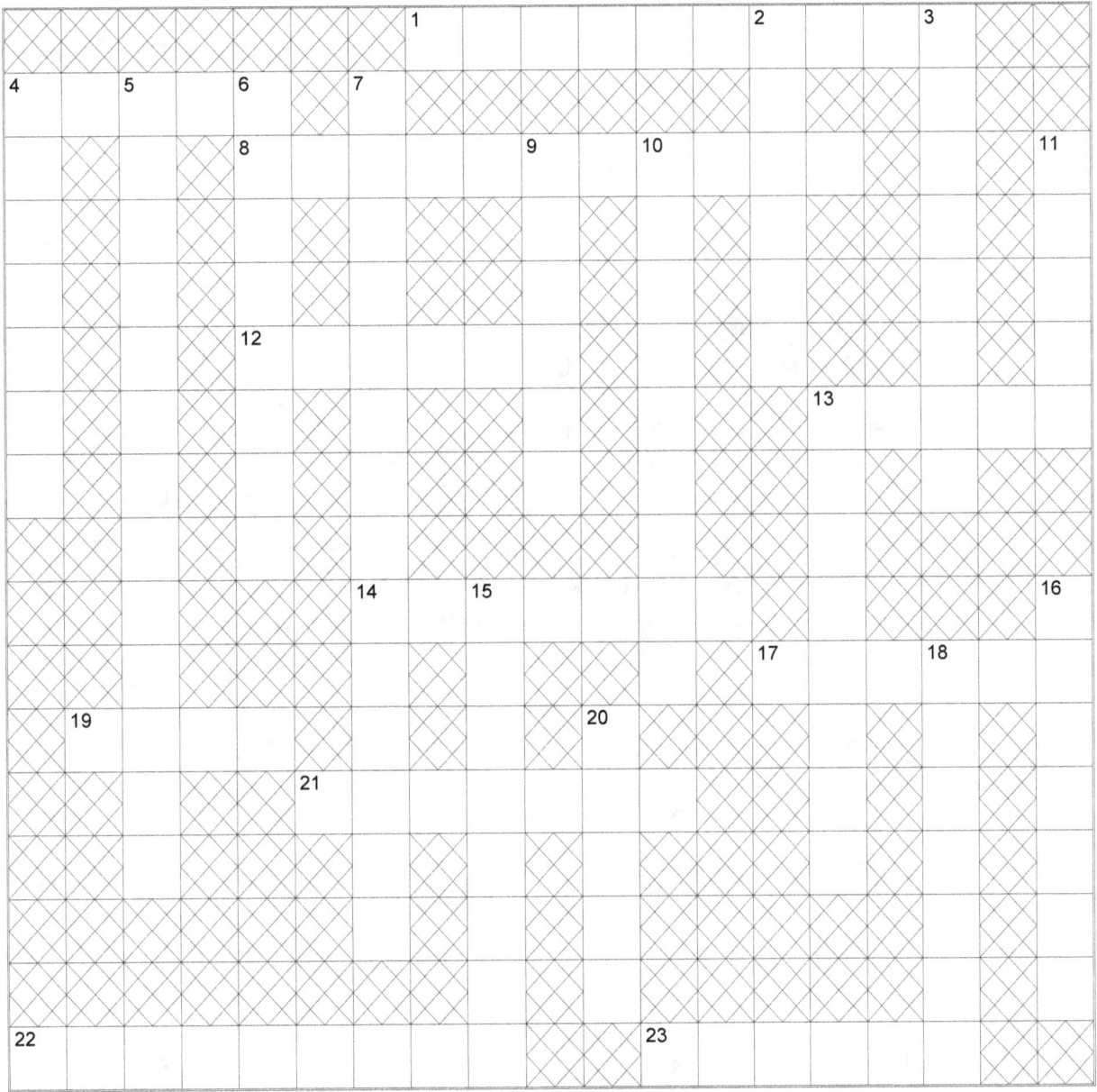

Across
1. Started; initiated
4. Easily understood; intelligible
8. Puzzling
12. Awaken or excite
13. Reverence
14. Hanging back or falling behind
17. Bell tower
19. On guard; watchful
21. Rebuked; scolded; put down
22. Trading goods or services without money
23. Uneasy feelings

Down
2. Reduced in amount
3. Hated
4. Merciful; indulgent
5. Sympathetic
6. The way in which a person behaves
7. Cheerlessly; gloomily
9. Passionate; displaying a strong enthusiasm
10. Unpaid service to another
11. Careful and shrewd
13. One whose welfare is promoted by another
15. Expressing great pleasure or self-satisfaction
16. Unjust use of absolute power
18. Unconsciously foolish
20. Danger

Johnny Tremain Vocabulary Crossword 3 Answer Key

Across
1. Started; initiated
4. Easily understood; intelligible
8. Puzzling
12. Awaken or excite
13. Reverence
14. Hanging back or falling behind
17. Bell tower
19. On guard; watchful
21. Rebuked; scolded; put down
22. Trading goods or services without money
23. Uneasy feelings

Down
2. Reduced in amount
3. Hated
4. Merciful; indulgent
5. Sympathetic
6. The way in which a person behaves
7. Cheerlessly; gloomily
9. Passionate; displaying a strong enthusiasm
10. Unpaid service to another
11. Careful and shrewd
13. One whose welfare is promoted by another
15. Expressing great pleasure or self-satisfaction
16. Unjust use of absolute power
18. Unconsciously foolish
20. Danger

Answers filled in grid:

Across:
1. INSTIGATED
4. LUCID
8. ENIGMATICAL
12. AROUSE
13. PIETY
14. LAGGARD
17. BELFRY
19. WARY
21. BERATED
22. BARTERING
23. QUALMS

Down:
2. ABATED
3. DETESTED
4. LENIENT
5. COMPASSIONATE
6. DEMEANOR
7. DISCONSOLATELY
9. ARDENT
10. INDEBTED
11. CANNY
13. PROTEGE
15. GLOATED
16. TYRANNY
18. FATUOUS
20. PERIL

Johnny Tremain Vocabulary Crossword 4

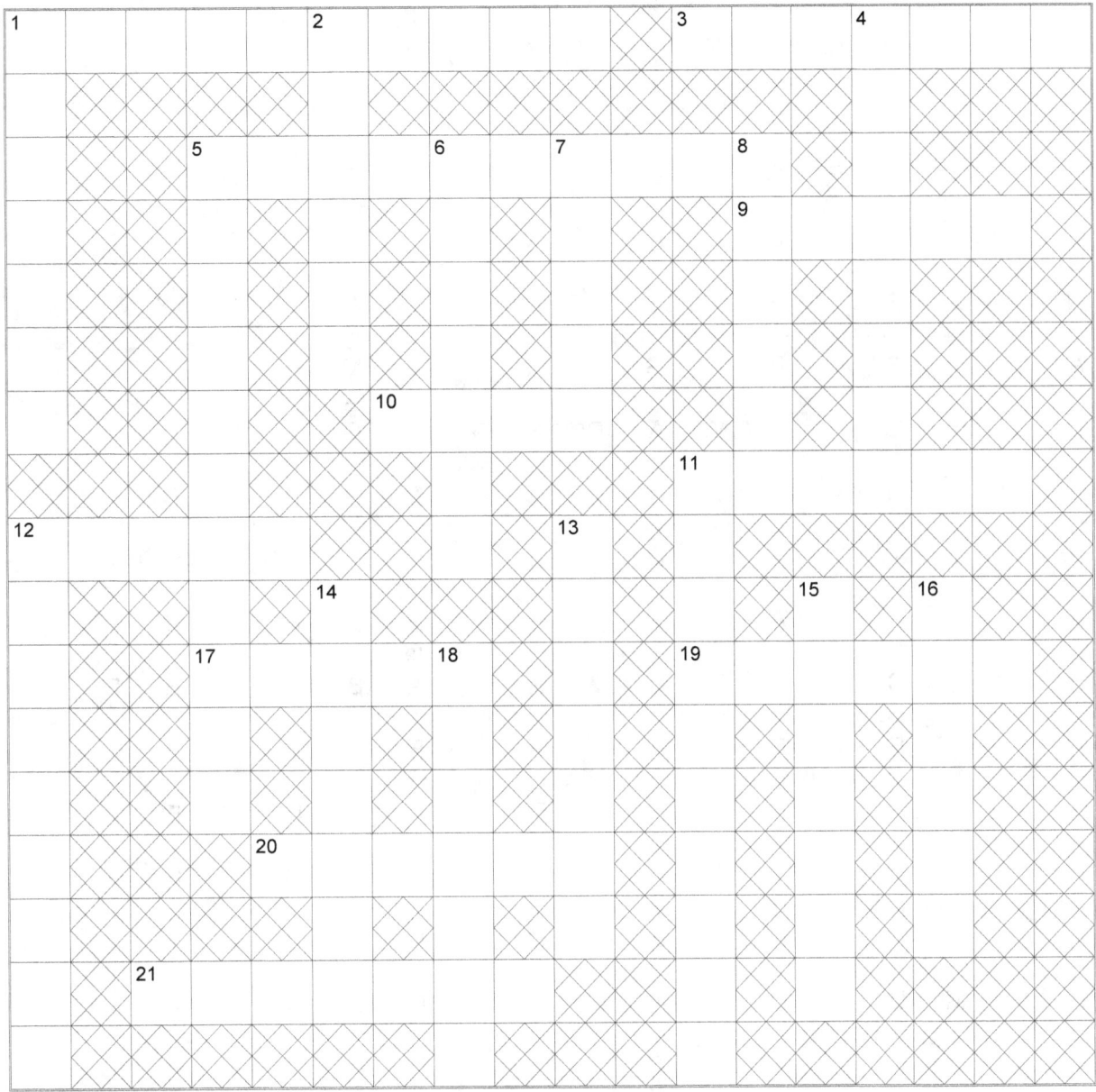

Across
1. Boastfully
3. Lacking vigor or energy
5. Having loss of muscular control & sensation
9. Easily understood; intelligible
10. On guard; watchful
11. Passionate; displaying a strong enthusiasm
12. Reverence
17. Relating to a citizen
19. Reduced in amount
20. A struggle or fight
21. Ordinary; boring

Down
1. A supply of weapons
2. Awaken or excite
4. Porcelain dish used for melting silver
5. Those who work in return for instruction
6. Hanging back or falling behind
7. Careful and shrewd
8. Uproar
11. Ghost
12. Taking advantage of others without useful return
13. Rebuked; scolded; put down
14. Turned away
15. Unconsciously foolish
16. Bell tower
18. Merciful; indulgent

Johnny Tremain Vocabulary Crossword 4 Answer Key

	1	2	3	4	5	6	7	8	9	10	11	12	13
1	A	R	R	O	G	A	N	T	L	Y		F	L	A	C	C	I	D

(Grid answers)

- 1 Across: ARROGANTLY
- 3 Across: FLACCID
- 5 Across: APOPLECTIC
- 9 Across: LUCID
- 10 Across: WARY
- 11 Across: ARDENT
- 12 Across: PIETY
- 17 Across: CIVIL
- 19 Across: ABATED
- 20 Across: STRIFE
- 21 Across: MUNDANE

- 1 Down: ARSENAL
- 2 Down: ROUSE
- 4 Down: CRUCIBLE
- 5 Down: APPRENTICES
- 6 Down: LAGGING
- 7 Down: CANNY
- 8 Down: CLAMOR
- 11 Down: APPARITION
- 13 Down: BERATED
- 14 Down: AVERTED
- 15 Down: FATUOUS
- 16 Down: BELFRY
- 18 Down: LENIENT

Across
1. Boastfully
3. Lacking vigor or energy
5. Having loss of muscular control & sensation
9. Easily understood; intelligible
10. On guard; watchful
11. Passionate; displaying a strong enthusiasm
12. Reverence
17. Relating to a citizen
19. Reduced in amount
20. A struggle or fight
21. Ordinary; boring

Down
1. A supply of weapons
2. Awaken or excite
4. Porcelain dish used for melting silver
5. Those who work in return for instruction
6. Hanging back or falling behind
7. Careful and shrewd
8. Uproar
11. Ghost
12. Taking advantage of others without useful return
13. Rebuked; scolded; put down
14. Turned away
15. Unconsciously foolish
16. Bell tower
18. Merciful; indulgent

Johnny Tremain Vocabulary Juggle Letters 1

1. NINVIELBCI = 1. _____
   Unconquerable

2. EEARVTD = 2. _____
   Turned away

3. DDPATDIIEAL = 3. _____
   Broken-down

4. PITCACOPLE = 4. _____
   Having loss of muscular control & sensation

5. DREROVPE = 5. _____
   Found fault with

6. DERNAT = 6. _____
   Passionate; displaying a strong enthusiasm

7. DETAAB = 7. _____
   Reduced in amount

8. LTEAHREE = 8. _____
   Airy; fragile

9. GREELTEBLIN = 9. _____
   Eager to fight; hostile

10. TABUTNROEPR =10. _____
    Swelling outward; bulging

11. ETYPI =11. _____
    Reverence

12. BCCEIRLU =12. _____
    Porcelain dish used for melting silver

13. TONAESR =13. _____
    Betrayal of one's country

14. ORTNYLAGRA =14. _____
    Boastfully

15. EBRMLCIPYEPTI =15. _____
    Not noticeably

Johnny Tremain Vocabulary Juggle Letters 1 Answer Key

1. NINVIELBCI = 1. INVINCIBLE
   Unconquerable

2. EEARVTD = 2. AVERTED
   Turned away

3. DDPATDIIEAL = 3. DILAPIDATED
   Broken-down

4. PITCACOPLE = 4. APOPLECTIC
   Having loss of muscular control & sensation

5. DREROVPE = 5. REPROVED
   Found fault with

6. DERNAT = 6. ARDENT
   Passionate; displaying a strong enthusiasm

7. DETAAB = 7. ABATED
   Reduced in amount

8. LTEAHREE = 8. ETHEREAL
   Airy; fragile

9. GREELTEBLIN = 9. BELLIGERENT
   Eager to fight; hostile

10. TABUTNROEPR =10. PROTUBERANT
    Swelling outward; bulging

11. ETYPI =11. PIETY
    Reverence

12. BCCEIRLU =12. CRUCIBLE
    Porcelain dish used for melting silver

13. TONAESR =13. TREASON
    Betrayal of one's country

14. ORTNYLAGRA =14. ARROGANTLY
    Boastfully

15. EBRMLCIPYEPTI =15. IMPERCEPTIBLY
    Not noticeably

Johnny Tremain Vocabulary Juggle Letters 2

1. NRSEGAVIEC = 1. _____
   Reasons for protest; complaints

2. ENEDOPAMR = 2. _____
   A public place for walking

3. UAMLQS = 3. _____
   Uneasy feelings

4. GRETOEEP = 4. _____
   One whose welfare is promoted by another

5. ALIMTRA = 5. _____
   Relating to war

6. MANLLBATEE = 6. _____
   Regrettable

7. RNOUBPERTTA = 7. _____
   Swelling outward; bulging

8. OERRICSNUINT = 8. _____
   An open revolt

9. LYACDRILO = 9. _____
   Sincerely; warmly

10. AWRY = 10. _____
    On guard; watchful

11. YMSRPXOA = 11. _____
    A spasm or fit

12. PPAITRIONA = 12. _____
    Ghost

13. EITOGLINR = 13. _____
    Standing idly about; lingering aimlessly

14. CUOLTUPISNI = 14. _____
    Precise; scrupulous

15. UIPQDE = 15. _____
    Felt wounded pride

Johnny Tremain Vocabulary Juggle Letters 2 Answer Key

1. NRSEGAVIEC = 1. GRIEVANCES
   Reasons for protest; complaints

2. ENEDOPAMR = 2. PROMENADE
   A public place for walking

3. UAMLQS = 3. QUALMS
   Uneasy feelings

4. GRETOEEP = 4. PROTEGEE
   One whose welfare is promoted by another

5. ALIMTRA = 5. MARTIAL
   Relating to war

6. MANLLBATEE = 6. LAMENTABLE
   Regrettable

7. RNOUBPERTTA = 7. PROTUBERANT
   Swelling outward; bulging

8. OERRICSNUINT = 8. INSURRECTION
   An open revolt

9. LYACDRILO = 9. CORDIALLY
   Sincerely; warmly

10. AWRY =10. WARY
    On guard; watchful

11. YMSRPXOA =11. PAROXYSM
    A spasm or fit

12. PPAITRIONA =12. APPARITION
    Ghost

13. EITOGLINR =13. LOITERING
    Standing idly about; lingering aimlessly

14. CUOLTUPISNI =14. PUNCTILIOUS
    Precise; scrupulous

15. UIPQDE =15. PIQUED
    Felt wounded pride

Johnny Tremain Vocabulary Juggle Letters 3

1. IUCLD = 1. _____
   Easily understood; intelligible

2. NOMEERAD = 2. _____
   The way in which a person behaves

3. EEMNAPODR = 3. _____
   A public place for walking

4. LOINYDACLSSTOE = 4. _____
   Cheerlessly; gloomily

5. TRAROYO = 5. _____
   Relating to public speaking

6. LPREI = 6. _____
   Danger

7. OPGDRSOIULIY = 7. _____
   In an impressively great way

8. SOFUUTA = 8. _____
   Unconsciously foolish

9. EREPODRV = 9. _____
   Found fault with

10. NBTTELUUR = 10. _____
    Violently agitated or disturbed

11. RTEOTUBNRPA = 11. _____
    Swelling outward; bulging

12. CRHEITE = 12. _____
    Misbeliever; one who holds controversial opinions

13. AMIARLT = 13. _____
    Relating to war

14. EERERTVD = 14. _____
    Returned to a former condition

15. ESARANL = 15. _____
    A supply of weapons

Johnny Tremain Vocabulary Juggle Letters 3 Answer Key

1. IUCLD = 1. LUCID
Easily understood; intelligible

2. NOMEERAD = 2. DEMEANOR
The way in which a person behaves

3. EEMNAPODR = 3. PROMENADE
A public place for walking

4. LOINYDACLSSTOE = 4. DISCONSOLATELY
Cheerlessly; gloomily

5. TRAROYO = 5. ORATORY
Relating to public speaking

6. LPREI = 6. PERIL
Danger

7. OPGDRSOIULIY = 7. PRODIGIOUSLY
In an impressively great way

8. SOFUUTA = 8. FATUOUS
Unconsciously foolish

9. EREPODRV = 9. REPROVED
Found fault with

10. NBTTELUUR = 10. TURBULENT
Violently agitated or disturbed

11. RTEOTUBNRPA = 11. PROTUBERANT
Swelling outward; bulging

12. CRHEITE = 12. HERETIC
Misbeliever; one who holds controversial opinions

13. AMIARLT = 13. MARTIAL
Relating to war

14. EERERTVD = 14. REVERTED
Returned to a former condition

15. ESARANL = 15. ARSENAL
A supply of weapons

Johnny Tremain Vocabulary Juggle Letters 4

1. SPICAAEMNSOOT = 1. _____
   Sympathetic

2. NYYNRTA = 2. _____
   Unjust use of absolute power

3. LCROAM = 3. _____
   Uproar

4. NOTOONICCC = 4. _____
   Food or beverage made of mixed ingredients

5. ETRCHIE = 5. _____
   Misbeliever; one who holds controversial opinions

6. NRAEDT = 6. _____
   Passionate; displaying a strong enthusiasm

7. RAGLDGA = 7. _____
   Hanging back or falling behind

8. PYETI = 8. _____
   Reverence

9. NIGLIDETLY = 9. _____
   In a hard-working manner

10. LETEBELNRIG =10. _____
    Eager to fight; hostile

11. CUNSOTIPULI =11. _____
    Precise; scrupulous

12. YDOLCILAR =12. _____
    Sincerely; warmly

13. ERDREETV =13. _____
    Returned to a former condition

14. TPGOEERE =14. _____
    One whose welfare is promoted by another

15. ROMNDAEE =15. _____
    The way in which a person behaves

Johnny Tremain Vocabulary Juggle Letters 4 Answer Key

1. SPICAAEMNSOOT = 1. COMPASSIONATE
Sympathetic

2. NYYNRTA = 2. TYRANNY
Unjust use of absolute power

3. LCROAM = 3. CLAMOR
Uproar

4. NOTOONICCC = 4. CONCOCTION
Food or beverage made of mixed ingredients

5. ETRCHIE = 5. HERETIC
Misbeliever; one who holds controversial opinions

6. NRAEDT = 6. ARDENT
Passionate; displaying a strong enthusiasm

7. RAGLDGA = 7. LAGGARD
Hanging back or falling behind

8. PYETI = 8. PIETY
Reverence

9. NIGLIDETLY = 9. DILIGENTLY
In a hard-working manner

10. LETEBELNRIG =10. BELLIGERENT
Eager to fight; hostile

11. CUNSOTIPULI =11. PUNCTILIOUS
Precise; scrupulous

12. YDOLCILAR =12. CORDIALLY
Sincerely; warmly

13. ERDREETV =13. REVERTED
Returned to a former condition

14. TPGOEERE =14. PROTEGEE
One whose welfare is promoted by another

15. ROMNDAEE =15. DEMEANOR
The way in which a person behaves

ABATED	Reduced in amount
APOPLECTIC	Having loss of muscular control & sensation
APPARITION	Ghost
APPRENTICES	Those who work in return for instruction
ARDENT	Passionate; displaying a strong enthusiasm
AROUSE	Awaken or excite

Copyrighted

ARROGANTLY	Boastfully
ARSENAL	A supply of weapons
AVERTED	Turned away
BARTERING	Trading goods or services without money
BELFRY	Bell tower
BELLIGERENT	Eager to fight; hostile

BERATED	Rebuked; scolded; put down
CANNY	Careful and shrewd
CIVIL	Relating to a citizen
CLAMOR	Uproar
COMPASSIONATE	Sympathetic
CONCOCTION	Food or beverage made of mixed ingredients

CORDIALLY	Sincerely; warmly
CRUCIBLE	Porcelain dish used for melting silver
CULTIVATE	To nurture
DEMEANOR	The way in which a person behaves
DETESTED	Hated
DIFFIDENTLY	Shyly; timidly

DILAPIDATED	Broken-down
DILIGENTLY	In a hard-working manner
DISCONSOLATELY	Cheerlessly; gloomily
DISPERSE	To scatter in different directions
ENIGMATICAL	Puzzling
ETHEREAL	Airy; fragile

FATUOUS	Unconsciously foolish
FLACCID	Lacking vigor or energy
GLOATING	Expressing great pleasure or self-satisfaction
GRIEVANCES	Reasons for protest; complaints
HERETIC	Misbeliever; one who holds controversial opinions
IMPERCEPTIBLY	Not noticeably

INCAPACITY	Inadequate strength or ability
INDENTURE	Unpaid service to another
INDOLENT	Habitually lazy
INSTIGATED	Started; initiated
INSURRECTION	An open revolt
INUNDATED	Overwhelmed; swamped

INVINCIBLE	Unconquerable
LAGGARD	Hanging back or falling behind
LAMENTABLE	Regrettable
LENIENT	Merciful; indulgent
LOITERING	Standing idly about; lingering aimlessly
LUCID	Easily understood; intelligible

MARTIAL	Relating to war
MUNDANE	Ordinary; boring
NONCHALANT	Unconcerned or indifferent
ORATORY	Relating to public speaking
PARASITIC	Taking advantage of others without useful return
PAROXYSM	A spasm or fit

PERIL	Danger
PIETY	Reverence
PIQUED	Felt wounded pride
PLACATE	To appease; make concessions
POULTICE	Dressing for a wound or injury
PRETENSE	A false action intended to deceive

PRODIGIOUSLY	In an impressively great way
PROMENADE	A public place for walking
PROTEGEE	One whose welfare is promoted by another
PROTUBERANT	Swelling outward; bulging
PUNCTILIOUS	Precise; scrupulous
QUALMS	Uneasy feelings

REPENTANCE	Remorse or contrition
REPROVED	Found fault with
REVERTED	Returned to a former condition
SEDITIOUS	Rebellious
SOLITARY	Alone
STRIFE	A struggle or fight

SUBDUED	Brought under control; quieted
SURFEITED	Saturated; overfilled
TEDIOUSLY	Slowly; in a boring manner
TENTATIVELY	Uncertainly; hesitantly
TREASON	Betrayal of one's country
TRIVIAL	Of little significance or value

TURBULENT	Violently agitated or disturbed
TYRANNY	Unjust use of absolute power
WARY	On guard; watchful
WAVERED	Showed indecision

Johnny Tremain Vocabulary

PIQUED	TRIVIAL	SEDITIOUS	FLACCID	INUNDATED
ENIGMATICAL	GRIEVANCES	PLACATE	PRODIGIOUSLY	DISPERSE
ABATED	TYRANNY	FREE SPACE	MUNDANE	WARY
ORATORY	PIETY	INCAPACITY	PROMENADE	TREASON
REPROVED	SURFEITED	TEDIOUSLY	BELFRY	AROUSE

Johnny Tremain Vocabulary

ARROGANTLY	CLAMOR	MARTIAL	LENIENT	INSTIGATED
CRUCIBLE	INVINCIBLE	BELLIGERENT	HERETIC	INDOLENT
PARASITIC	CULTIVATE	FREE SPACE	LUCID	DILAPIDATED
DISCONSOLATELY	LAMENTABLE	PROTUBERANT	REVERTED	PAROXYSM
TENTATIVELY	CIVIL	PROTEGEE	CORDIALLY	GLOATING

Johnny Tremain Vocabulary

WAVERED	SUBDUED	LAMENTABLE	AROUSE	TENTATIVELY
PRETENSE	BELLIGERENT	ARDENT	BELFRY	PLACATE
QUALMS	PROMENADE	FREE SPACE	DILAPIDATED	DEMEANOR
TYRANNY	PIETY	INDENTURE	GLOATING	REPENTANCE
SURFEITED	CIVIL	INSURRECTION	LUCID	PERIL

Johnny Tremain Vocabulary

PAROXYSM	CONCOCTION	LAGGARD	CULTIVATE	INVINCIBLE
CRUCIBLE	TREASON	FLACCID	WARY	COMPASSIONATE
DISPERSE	MUNDANE	FREE SPACE	INSTIGATED	SEDITIOUS
HERETIC	INUNDATED	MARTIAL	AVERTED	CORDIALLY
CANNY	PRODIGIOUSLY	POULTICE	BARTERING	TRIVIAL

Johnny Tremain Vocabulary

AVERTED	CORDIALLY	MUNDANE	REPENTANCE	CONCOCTION
PRETENSE	INVINCIBLE	GLOATING	LAGGARD	PARASITIC
PRODIGIOUSLY	ARSENAL	FREE SPACE	WAVERED	TREASON
PIQUED	DIFFIDENTLY	DEMEANOR	TRIVIAL	APPARITION
QUALMS	TURBULENT	GRIEVANCES	CANNY	POULTICE

Johnny Tremain Vocabulary

LUCID	BELLIGERENT	ABATED	ARDENT	DILAPIDATED
SEDITIOUS	STRIFE	FLACCID	TYRANNY	ENIGMATICAL
FATUOUS	DISPERSE	FREE SPACE	DILIGENTLY	CIVIL
ETHEREAL	CULTIVATE	ORATORY	DETESTED	COMPASSIONATE
SOLITARY	CLAMOR	ARROGANTLY	TEDIOUSLY	PERIL

Johnny Tremain Vocabulary

DIFFIDENTLY	INVINCIBLE	ARSENAL	CULTIVATE	BELLIGERENT
TYRANNY	INDOLENT	ORATORY	INSTIGATED	REVERTED
APPARITION	IMPERCEPTIBLY	FREE SPACE	CANNY	APPRENTICES
REPROVED	SUBDUED	SOLITARY	COMPASSIONATE	PLACATE
TRIVIAL	QUALMS	SEDITIOUS	STRIFE	TURBULENT

Johnny Tremain Vocabulary

INDENTURE	WAVERED	WARY	CLAMOR	PUNCTILIOUS
TREASON	ABATED	BARTERING	MARTIAL	BELFRY
DETESTED	PROMENADE	FREE SPACE	ARROGANTLY	CORDIALLY
TEDIOUSLY	DILIGENTLY	CONCOCTION	CIVIL	PROTEGEE
REPENTANCE	POULTICE	AROUSE	LAMENTABLE	PAROXYSM

Johnny Tremain Vocabulary

CIVIL	COMPASSIONATE	QUALMS	ETHEREAL	TYRANNY
SURFEITED	APOPLECTIC	WAVERED	PERIL	SUBDUED
PIETY	INCAPACITY	FREE SPACE	DISCONSOLATELY	BELLIGERENT
PUNCTILIOUS	LAGGARD	ORATORY	PIQUED	DEMEANOR
INSURRECTION	IMPERCEPTIBLY	ARDENT	DETESTED	INDOLENT

Johnny Tremain Vocabulary

AVERTED	CRUCIBLE	FLACCID	PLACATE	HERETIC
FATUOUS	LUCID	CLAMOR	NONCHALANT	DISPERSE
SOLITARY	CULTIVATE	FREE SPACE	TREASON	CORDIALLY
TURBULENT	CONCOCTION	WARY	REPENTANCE	PRETENSE
PROMENADE	TENTATIVELY	APPRENTICES	INUNDATED	ARROGANTLY

Johnny Tremain Vocabulary

MUNDANE	LOITERING	AVERTED	LUCID	CULTIVATE
DIFFIDENTLY	BARTERING	LENIENT	APPARITION	TRIVIAL
PROMENADE	BERATED	FREE SPACE	IMPERCEPTIBLY	DILIGENTLY
TREASON	CIVIL	COMPASSIONATE	PRODIGIOUSLY	INSURRECTION
WAVERED	FLACCID	NONCHALANT	PERIL	TENTATIVELY

Johnny Tremain Vocabulary

MARTIAL	INDENTURE	TURBULENT	LAMENTABLE	INDOLENT
BELFRY	SOLITARY	WARY	LAGGARD	HERETIC
TEDIOUSLY	APOPLECTIC	FREE SPACE	SEDITIOUS	PROTEGEE
ENIGMATICAL	PRETENSE	PUNCTILIOUS	PIETY	DEMEANOR
CRUCIBLE	PROTUBERANT	ARDENT	REPENTANCE	DISCONSOLATELY

Johnny Tremain Vocabulary

POULTICE	INDENTURE	CONCOCTION	REVERTED	REPROVED
DILAPIDATED	PROTUBERANT	DEMEANOR	ENIGMATICAL	INSURRECTION
DILIGENTLY	TEDIOUSLY	FREE SPACE	APPARITION	LUCID
DETESTED	FLACCID	CORDIALLY	INVINCIBLE	DIFFIDENTLY
SOLITARY	INSTIGATED	TYRANNY	TURBULENT	LENIENT

Johnny Tremain Vocabulary

PRETENSE	PARASITIC	PERIL	LAMENTABLE	BELLIGERENT
REPENTANCE	PRODIGIOUSLY	ARDENT	PIETY	CANNY
ETHEREAL	TENTATIVELY	FREE SPACE	PIQUED	SURFEITED
MARTIAL	CRUCIBLE	CLAMOR	GRIEVANCES	STRIFE
INUNDATED	ARSENAL	INCAPACITY	WARY	FATUOUS

Johnny Tremain Vocabulary

INDOLENT	APOPLECTIC	MARTIAL	PRODIGIOUSLY	INUNDATED
ARDENT	PERIL	NONCHALANT	APPARITION	FATUOUS
SUBDUED	TYRANNY	FREE SPACE	PAROXYSM	INDENTURE
PARASITIC	REPROVED	PROTUBERANT	APPRENTICES	LOITERING
GLOATING	AROUSE	DILIGENTLY	ETHEREAL	POULTICE

Johnny Tremain Vocabulary

CONCOCTION	STRIFE	DEMEANOR	ABATED	SOLITARY
IMPERCEPTIBLY	PIETY	LENIENT	CANNY	CIVIL
SURFEITED	CLAMOR	FREE SPACE	BERATED	INSURRECTION
TREASON	WARY	GRIEVANCES	HERETIC	PROTEGEE
CRUCIBLE	INCAPACITY	QUALMS	TEDIOUSLY	ARROGANTLY

Johnny Tremain Vocabulary

INSTIGATED	CULTIVATE	STRIFE	DIFFIDENTLY	APPRENTICES
ABATED	CRUCIBLE	PLACATE	QUALMS	DETESTED
INDOLENT	BERATED	FREE SPACE	REPROVED	TRIVIAL
AROUSE	ARSENAL	PROTEGEE	COMPASSIONATE	ETHEREAL
SUBDUED	IMPERCEPTIBLY	DISPERSE	LAMENTABLE	SURFEITED

Johnny Tremain Vocabulary

PROMENADE	INSURRECTION	PUNCTILIOUS	MARTIAL	GLOATING
PIETY	BELLIGERENT	PAROXYSM	PRODIGIOUSLY	CLAMOR
SEDITIOUS	REPENTANCE	FREE SPACE	INUNDATED	MUNDANE
CANNY	DEMEANOR	INCAPACITY	NONCHALANT	CORDIALLY
INDENTURE	APOPLECTIC	WAVERED	TEDIOUSLY	ORATORY

Johnny Tremain Vocabulary

APOPLECTIC	SOLITARY	CRUCIBLE	ARDENT	REPENTANCE
QUALMS	SURFEITED	AROUSE	ENIGMATICAL	CORDIALLY
BELLIGERENT	COMPASSIONATE	FREE SPACE	PIQUED	PRETENSE
MARTIAL	ETHEREAL	PERIL	PROMENADE	PIETY
INVINCIBLE	FLACCID	INSURRECTION	WAVERED	CANNY

Johnny Tremain Vocabulary

TURBULENT	ARSENAL	CIVIL	LAGGARD	INUNDATED
DILIGENTLY	TEDIOUSLY	GRIEVANCES	BELFRY	NONCHALANT
ABATED	DETESTED	FREE SPACE	DISPERSE	INDOLENT
PRODIGIOUSLY	PAROXYSM	APPRENTICES	SUBDUED	INCAPACITY
CLAMOR	REPROVED	WARY	CONCOCTION	HERETIC

Johnny Tremain Vocabulary

DILAPIDATED	DILIGENTLY	SURFEITED	PLACATE	HERETIC
REPROVED	GRIEVANCES	DIFFIDENTLY	MARTIAL	TENTATIVELY
CLAMOR	LENIENT	FREE SPACE	MUNDANE	INDOLENT
DETESTED	REPENTANCE	STRIFE	APPRENTICES	APPARITION
PROMENADE	QUALMS	TEDIOUSLY	AROUSE	ORATORY

Johnny Tremain Vocabulary

CORDIALLY	ARDENT	CONCOCTION	BARTERING	TRIVIAL
PIETY	ARROGANTLY	CRUCIBLE	INDENTURE	LOITERING
INSTIGATED	PRETENSE	FREE SPACE	ABATED	COMPASSIONATE
POULTICE	SEDITIOUS	BELFRY	BERATED	LAGGARD
ETHEREAL	DISPERSE	PIQUED	WAVERED	APOPLECTIC

Johnny Tremain Vocabulary

PRODIGIOUSLY	COMPASSIONATE	NONCHALANT	PROTEGEE	INUNDATED
INVINCIBLE	APPRENTICES	INDOLENT	REPENTANCE	INSURRECTION
DIFFIDENTLY	PUNCTILIOUS	FREE SPACE	PAROXYSM	ABATED
WARY	ENIGMATICAL	TURBULENT	DILIGENTLY	PRETENSE
WAVERED	GLOATING	LENIENT	ETHEREAL	ARSENAL

Johnny Tremain Vocabulary

BERATED	DISPERSE	TRIVIAL	CRUCIBLE	DETESTED
DEMEANOR	CLAMOR	FATUOUS	LAMENTABLE	BELFRY
LOITERING	FLACCID	FREE SPACE	PIQUED	TEDIOUSLY
PROTUBERANT	TREASON	SEDITIOUS	BARTERING	POULTICE
TYRANNY	TENTATIVELY	LAGGARD	SUBDUED	HERETIC

Johnny Tremain Vocabulary

APOPLECTIC	BARTERING	INDOLENT	TYRANNY	CANNY
MUNDANE	CIVIL	SURFEITED	ORATORY	ENIGMATICAL
TREASON	PAROXYSM	FREE SPACE	NONCHALANT	BELFRY
LAMENTABLE	INVINCIBLE	APPARITION	INSURRECTION	PARASITIC
DEMEANOR	FATUOUS	DILAPIDATED	ETHEREAL	REPROVED

Johnny Tremain Vocabulary

ABATED	PRODIGIOUSLY	APPRENTICES	INCAPACITY	AROUSE
TEDIOUSLY	PIQUED	PROTUBERANT	CULTIVATE	WAVERED
INUNDATED	CONCOCTION	FREE SPACE	GLOATING	SUBDUED
DISPERSE	CRUCIBLE	LUCID	COMPASSIONATE	INDENTURE
DETESTED	PROMENADE	FLACCID	CORDIALLY	SOLITARY

Johnny Tremain Vocabulary

CANNY	ARROGANTLY	SUBDUED	LOITERING	CONCOCTION
INSURRECTION	REPENTANCE	BELLIGERENT	CIVIL	ABATED
AVERTED	TEDIOUSLY	FREE SPACE	PROTUBERANT	TRIVIAL
ARSENAL	ORATORY	DISCONSOLATELY	ENIGMATICAL	GLOATING
DISPERSE	PRODIGIOUSLY	REPROVED	PIQUED	REVERTED

Johnny Tremain Vocabulary

POULTICE	PROMENADE	PROTEGEE	DILIGENTLY	WAVERED
DEMEANOR	PARASITIC	PERIL	DILAPIDATED	APPRENTICES
ETHEREAL	SURFEITED	FREE SPACE	QUALMS	APPARITION
INCAPACITY	PLACATE	CORDIALLY	COMPASSIONATE	PUNCTILIOUS
APOPLECTIC	LAMENTABLE	INSTIGATED	TREASON	HERETIC

Johnny Tremain Vocabulary

BARTERING	REVERTED	PROTEGEE	DISPERSE	MUNDANE
WARY	REPENTANCE	DETESTED	CULTIVATE	PROMENADE
TURBULENT	APOPLECTIC	FREE SPACE	TENTATIVELY	POULTICE
SURFEITED	SEDITIOUS	CLAMOR	ORATORY	STRIFE
PUNCTILIOUS	HERETIC	PERIL	PARASITIC	PIETY

Johnny Tremain Vocabulary

PRODIGIOUSLY	AVERTED	CANNY	LOITERING	DISCONSOLATELY
CRUCIBLE	PIQUED	BELFRY	INSTIGATED	ARDENT
PRETENSE	NONCHALANT	FREE SPACE	APPARITION	INSURRECTION
TRIVIAL	MARTIAL	ETHEREAL	DILIGENTLY	INDENTURE
PLACATE	LUCID	CIVIL	DEMEANOR	ARROGANTLY

Johnny Tremain Vocabulary

BELLIGERENT	REVERTED	ARDENT	PIQUED	AVERTED
INVINCIBLE	FLACCID	SUBDUED	WARY	DILAPIDATED
SEDITIOUS	APPRENTICES	FREE SPACE	DISCONSOLATELY	CLAMOR
ARROGANTLY	APPARITION	CANNY	PROMENADE	DIFFIDENTLY
POULTICE	INSURRECTION	TYRANNY	INUNDATED	HERETIC

Johnny Tremain Vocabulary

TURBULENT	BELFRY	NONCHALANT	WAVERED	CONCOCTION
REPENTANCE	INDENTURE	MARTIAL	CRUCIBLE	TRIVIAL
DILIGENTLY	INDOLENT	FREE SPACE	ENIGMATICAL	DEMEANOR
INSTIGATED	BARTERING	IMPERCEPTIBLY	PLACATE	PIETY
GRIEVANCES	PROTUBERANT	LENIENT	ARSENAL	PRETENSE

www.ingramcontent.com/pod-product-compliance
Lightning Source LLC
Chambersburg PA
CBHW081452070526
44586CB00019B/2328